THE LITTLE BIG BOOK FOR
MOMS

This book belongs to:

Melinda Miller on

her First Mother's Day

May 9, 2010.

With love,

Nancy Motz

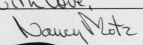

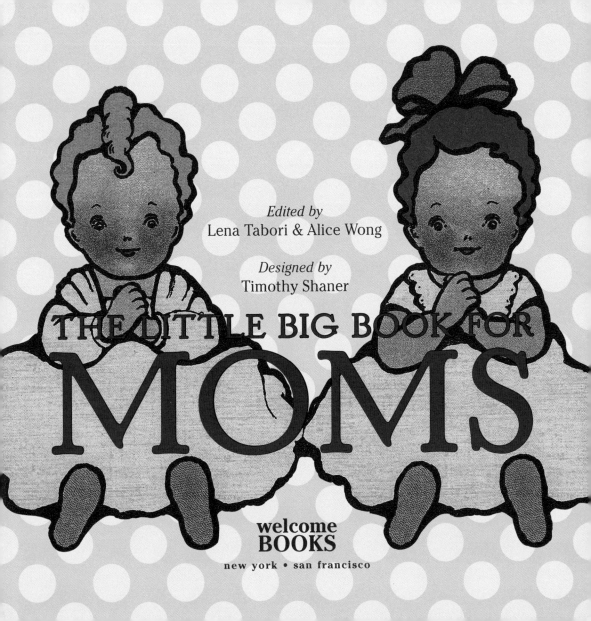

Edited by
Lena Tabori & Alice Wong

Designed by
Timothy Shaner

THE LITTLE BIG BOOK FOR
MOMS

welcome
BOOKS

new york • san francisco

Published in 2010 by Welcome Books®
An imprint of Welcome Enterprises, Inc.
6 West 18th Street, New York, NY 10011
(212) 989-3200; Fax (212) 989-3205
www.welcomebooks.com

Fairy tales retold by Katrina Fried
Jacket illustrations by Hilda Austin
Finger games illustrations by Megan Halsey
Editorial Assistance by Natasha Tabori Fried and Akasemi Newsome

Manufactured by WKT Co. Ltd in Hong Kong, China
November 2009
Job #LBBM2.1

Library of Congress Cataloging-in-Publication Data
The little big book for moms / edited by Lena Tabori and Alice Wong ; designed by Timothy
Shaner.
          p. cm.
  Summary: A collection of traditional tales, nursery ryhmes, songs, literary excerpts,
poems, finger games, recipes and more.
1. Children's literature. [1. Literature-Collections.] I. Tabori, Lena. II. Wong, Alice.
PZ5.L7175 2000
649'.5-dc21

ISBN-978-1-59962-075-6

Printed in China

FIRST EDITION / 10 9 8 7 6 5 4 3 2

Contents

Contents

Nursery Rhymes

Songs

Contents

You too, my mother,
  read my rhymes
For love of unforgotten times,
And you may chance
  to hear once more
The little feet along the floor.

—Robert Louis Stevenson

Foreword

My two are grown, 39 and 37, Natasha and Katrina. The days of their being little are long gone—but no matter, that didn't keep them out of this book. Most of the recipes date from when they were small. There never was a more successful birthday than when they decorated cupcakes with their friends and brought all the extras to kindergarten to celebrate again the next day. And that's not all: Katrina rewrote all the classic fairy tales that appear here; amplifying those parts she loved best as a child and reducing others. Ten years ago, when we were working on the first edition, she called and read me pieces of what she'd just finished writing, and I wept (how foolish mothers are!), and listened as my daughter reminded me how magical both she and the fairy tales are. She does such good papa bear, mama bear, and baby bear voices that we've put a podcast on the mom's mini-site: www.welcomebooks.com/moms

Natasha has been a collector of children's illustrations since she was a child. For this book, she dug into her volumes of old children's books, and then she and Alice searched paper ephemera shows all over New England while I combed the West Coast. The result is the adorable and beautiful collection of art found within these pages.

Alice has infinite patience with her little ones. I will confess I did not always, with mine. But I do remember how the three of us always found peace and coziness when we cuddled up on the sofa with stories, or were busy for hours up to our elbows in cookie dough. It's clear to me now that if this little book had existed then, it would have been my treasure; it would have been as well thumbed as my copy of *What to Expect When You're Expecting* was by the time Natasha was born. And there would have been many nights when Natasha and Katrina would have heard me ask that old familiar question, "What shall we read tonight?" and the answer would have been, "Mom's Book."

—Lena Tabori

This book was conceived in a middle-of-the-night haze when my second daughter was a fussy, hungry, and loud little bundle. It is hard to believe but my girls are 13, 11, and 7 now. So big! The days of getting messy with soap bubbles or huffing and puffing as the big bad wolf, seem so long ago. Except every once in a while, it all comes back in special moments: bouncing my baby nephew to "Animal Fair" and realizing it still works as a baby soother; watching my girls spin and spin their little cousins to Ring-Around-the-Rosie; hearing my husband reprimand the kids— "No more monkeys jumping on the bed!" I come from a big, close extended family, and my brother and all my cousins are having little ones now. It fills me with amazement to watch my girls, the designated family babysitters, toss out all the tried-and-true songs, rhymes, and activities to entertain the littlest ones in the family now.

It is bittersweet to acknowledge my three are "all grown up," but this book brings back such wonderful memories. Phoebe's first bubbling laughs came when I moved her hands to do "Pat-a-Cake" with her older sister. When I introduced "Five Little Monkeys" to Chi Chi, she squealed with delight every time I enacted "bumped his head." "Old MacDonald" was Chi Chi and Sylvia's first duet. Chi Chi sang the verses, and year-old Sylvia proudly did the ee-ai-ee-ai-oh's. Once, when Sylvia was resisting sleep, I stood down the hall from their room and listened while Chi Chi did an entire repertoire, first of songs and then nursery rhymes, to comfort her baby sister. I was amazed by what she remembered, and Sylvia was so impressed she fell asleep.

We moved to fairy tales and poetry when they were two or three years old. "The Three Billy Goats Gruff" was always a favorite, mostly because the three of them love stomping across the bridge (Phoebe was always trying to keep up); and big bad wolves, whether in "Little Red Riding Hood" or "The Three Little Pigs" were always a big hit. Sylvia never quite sat still for poetry but Chi Chi and

Phoebe both loved "Wynken, Blynken and Nod" as a nighttime favorite. "Jabberwocky" and "Life Doesn't Frighten Me" moved into their world when they fell in love with nonsense words and scary things.

I am constantly amazed by the amount of energy children have. There were days when we started with play dough and ended with hand shadows, with a million things in between. The girls were never happier than when they had my or their father's full attention. Papa was always good for some amazing paper hats or airplanes. And even though I have never been much of a baker, I got a few great recipes from Lena, and spent messy and delicious afternoons with the girls and a lot of flour.

It has been over a decade since I first pondered motherhood. The nervous excitement, the overwhelming wonder and love . . . such a range of feelings is brought back to me by the collection of essays also found in this book. An amazing group of women write beautifully and wisely about their experiences as mothers. Gail Greiner writes of her fears of not being a supermom, and Terry Strother about slowing down to enjoy her four-year-old. Anne Lamott writes that there are places in the heart you don't even know exist until you love a child.

There is so much to enjoy in the precious early years. I look back at them and marvel and miss the lovely "bubble" my girls and I created with a few beloved songs and stories and simple activities. Hold on to your little ones. Create that special world of love and fun with them. They grow up too fast! Lena and I created this book because we love having children in our lives, and being mothers is such an important part of our existence. We know that this little gem in your hand, filled with the BEST of childhood, will give you and your little ones hours of fun, laughter, and enjoyment, and lots and lots of wonderful memories to treasure.

—Alice Wong

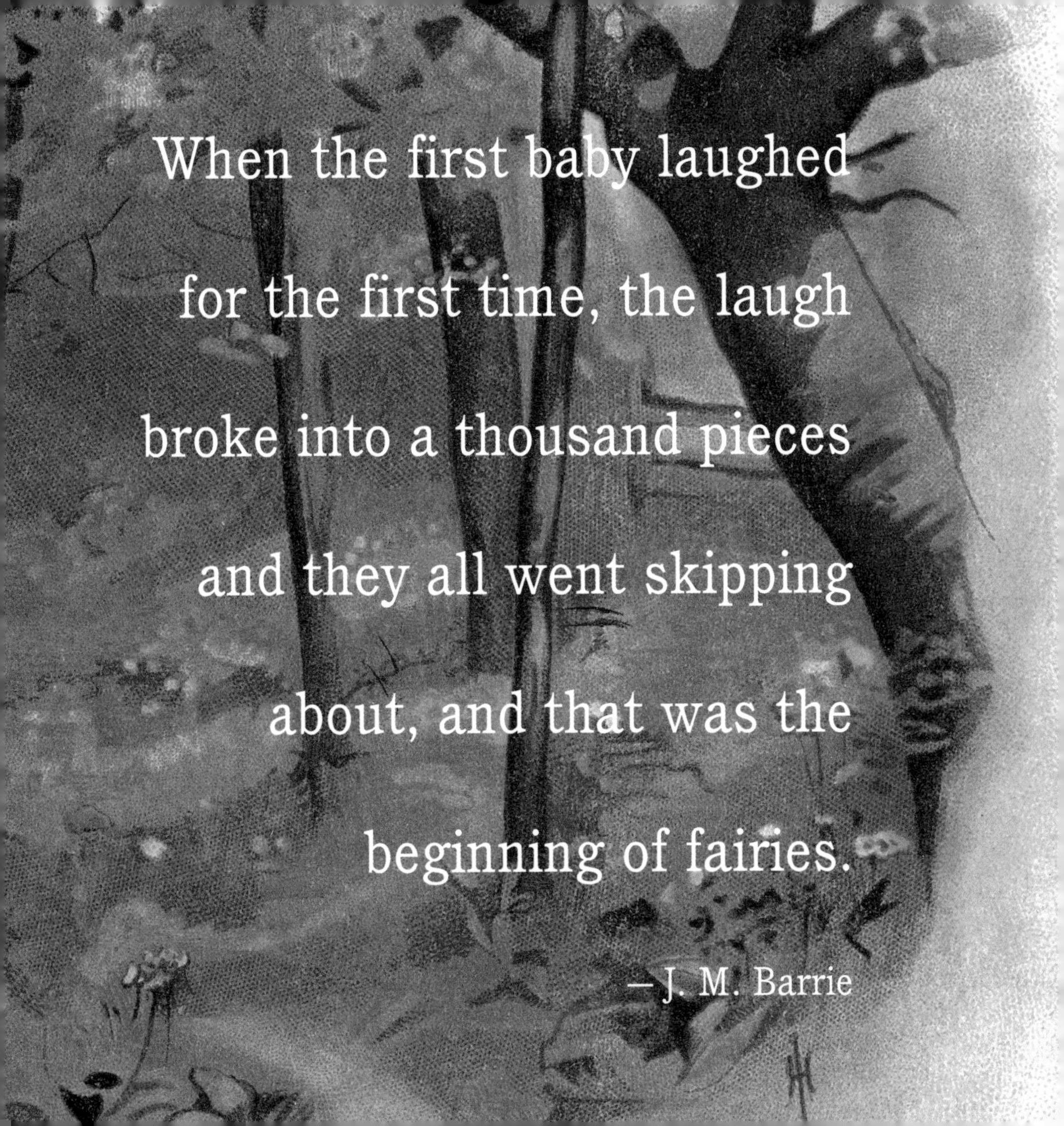

When the first baby laughed

for the first time, the laugh

broke into a thousand pieces

and they all went skipping

about, and that was the

beginning of fairies.

— J. M. Barrie

There Was a Child Went Forth
Walt Whitman

There was a child went forth every day,
And the first object he look'd upon, that object he became,
And that object became part of him for the day
    or a certain part of the day,
Or for many years or stretching eyeles of years.

The early lilacs became part of this child,
And grass and white and red morning-glories,
    and white and red clover, and the song of
    the phoebe-bird,
And the Third-month lambs and the sow's pink-faint litter,
    and the mare's foal and the cow's calf,
And the noisy brood of the barnyard or by
    the mire of the pondside,
And the fish suspending themselves so curiously
    below there, and the beautiful curious liquid,
And the water-plants with their graceful flat heads,
    all became part of him.

His own parents, he that had father'd him and she
    that had conceiv'd him in her womb and birth'd him,
They gave this child more of themselves than that,
They gave him afterward every day, they became part of him.

Charlotte's Web

E. B. White

Next morning when the first light came into the sky and the sparrows stirred in the trees, when the cows rattled their chains and the rooster crowed and the early automobiles went whispering along the road, Wilbur awoke and looked for Charlotte. He saw her up overhead in a corner near the back of his pen. She was very quiet. Her eight legs were spread wide. She seemed to have shrunk during the night. Next to her, attached to the ceiling, Wilbur saw a curious object. It was a sort of sac, or cocoon. It was peach-colored and looked as though it were made of cotton candy.

"Are you awake, Charlotte?" he said softly.

"Yes," came the answer.

"What is that nifty little thing? Did you make it?"

"I did indeed," replied Charlotte in a weak voice.

"Is it a plaything?"

"Plaything? I should say not. It is my egg sac, my *magnum opus*."

"I don't know what a magnum opus is," said Wilbur.

"That's Latin," explained Charlotte. "It means 'great work.' This egg sac is my great work—the finest thing I have ever made."

"What's inside it?" asked Wilbur. "Eggs?"

"Five hundred and fourteen of them," she replied.

"Five hundred and fourteen?" said Wilbur. "You're kidding."

"No, I'm not. I counted them. I got started counting, so I kept on—just to keep my mind occupied."

"It's a perfectly beautiful egg sac," said Wilbur, feeling as happy as though he had constructed it himself.

"Yes, it *is* pretty," replied Charlotte, patting the sac with her two front legs. "Anyway, I can guarantee that it is strong. It's made out of the toughest material I have. It is also waterproof. The eggs are inside and will be warm and dry."

"Charlotte," said Wilbur dreamily, "are you really going to have five hundred and fourteen children?"

"If nothing happens, yes," she said. "Of course, they won't show up till next spring."

Patiently Wilbur awaited the end of winter and the coming of the little spiders. Life is always a rich and steady time when you are waiting for something to happen or to hatch. The winter ended at last.

One fine sunny morning, after breakfast, Wilbur stood watching his precious sac. He wasn't thinking of anything much. As he stood there, he noticed something move. He stepped closer and stared. A tiny spider crawled from the sac. It was no bigger than a grain of sand, no bigger than the head of a pin. Its body was grey with a black stripe underneath. Its legs were grey and tan. It looked just like Charlotte.

Wilbur trembled all over when he saw it. The little spider waved at him. Then Wilbur looked more closely. Two more little spiders crawled out and waved. They climbed round and round on the sac, exploring their new world.

Then three more little spiders. Then eight. Then ten. Charlotte's children were here at last.

Wilbur's heart pounded. He began to squeal. Then he raced in circles, kicking manure into the air. Then he turned a back flip. Then he planted his front feet and came to a stop in front of Charlotte's children.

"Hello, there!" he said.

The first spider said hello, but its voice was so small Wilbur couldn't hear it.

"I am an old friend of your mother's," said Wilbur. "I'm glad to see you. Are you all right? Is everything all right?"

The little spiders waved their forelegs at him. Wilbur could see by the way they acted that they were glad to see him.

"Is there anything I can get you? Is there anything you need?"

The young spiders just waved. For several days and several nights they crawled here and there, up and down, around and about, waving at Wilbur, trailing tiny draglines behind them, and exploring their home. There were dozens and dozens of them. Wilbur couldn't count them, but he knew that he had a great many new friends. They grew quite rapidly. Soon each was as big as a BB shot. They made tiny webs near the sac.

Then came a quiet morning when Mr. Zuckerman opened a door on the north side. A warm draft of rising air blew softly through the barn cellar. The air smelled of the damp earth, of the spruce woods, of the sweet spring-

time. The baby spiders felt the warm updraft. One spider climbed to the top of the fence. Then it did something that came as a great surprise to Wilbur. The spider stood on its head, pointed its spinnerets in the air, and let loose a cloud of fine silk. The silk formed a balloon. As Wilbur watched, the spider let go of the fence and rose into the air.

"Good-bye!" it said, as it sailed through the doorway.

"Wait a minute!" screamed Wilbur. "Where do you think you're going?"

But the spider was already out of sight. Then another baby spider crawled to the top of the fence, stood on its head, made a balloon, and sailed away. Then another spider. Then another. The air was soon filled with tiny balloons, each balloon carrying a spider.

Wilbur was frantic. Charlotte's babies were disappearing at a great rate.

"Come back, children!" he cried.

"Good-bye!" they called. "Good-bye, good-bye!"

At last one little spider took time enough to stop and talk to Wilbur before making its balloon.

"We're leaving here on the warm updraft. This is our moment for setting forth. We are aeronauts and we are going out into the world to make webs for ourselves."

"But *where*?" asked Wilbur.

"Wherever the wind takes us. High, low. Near, far. East, west. North, south. We take to the breeze, we go as we please."

Are *all* of you going?" asked Wilbur. "You can't *all* go. I would be left alone, with no friends. Your mother wouldn't want that to happen, I'm sure."

The air was now so full of balloonists that the barn cellar looked almost as though a mist had gathered. Balloons by the dozen were rising, circling, and drifting away through the door, sailing off on the gentle winds. Cries of "Good-bye, good-bye, good-bye!" came weakly to Wilbur's ears. He couldn't bear to watch any more. In sorrow he sank to the ground and closed his eyes. This seemed like the end of the world, to be deserted by Charlotte's children. Wilbur cried himself to sleep.

When he woke it was late afternoon. He looked at the egg sac. It was empty. He looked into the air. The balloonists were gone. Then he walked drearily to the doorway, where Charlotte's web used to be. He was standing there, thinking of her, when he heard a small voice.

"Salutations!" it said. "I'm up here."

"So am I," said another tiny voice.

"So am I," said a third voice. "Three of us are staying. We like this place, and we like *you*."

Wilbur looked up. At the top of the doorway three small webs were being constructed. On each web, working busily was one of charlotte's daughters.

"Can I take this to mean," asked Wilbur, "that you have definitely decided to live here in the barn cellar, and that I am going to have *three* friends?"

"You can indeed," said the spiders.

"What are your names, please?" asked Wilbur, trembling with joy.

"I'll tell you my name," replied the first little spider, "if you'll tell me why you are trembling."

"I'm trembling with joy," said Wilbur.

"Then my name is Joy," said the first spider.

"What was my mother's middle initial?" asked the second spider.

"A," said Wilbur.

"Then my name is Aranea," said the spider.

"How about me?" asked the third spider. "Will you just pick out a nice sensible name for me—something not too long, not too fancy, and not too dumb?"

Wilbur thought hard.

"Nellie?" he suggested.

"Fine, I like that very much," said the third spider. "You may call me Nellie." She daintily fastened her orb line to the next spoke of the web.

Wilbur's heart brimmed with happiness. He felt that he should make a short speech on this very important occasion.

"Joy! Aranea! Nellie!" he began. "Welcome to the barn cellar. You have chosen a hallowed doorway from which to string your webs. I think it is only fair to tell you that I was devoted to your mother. I owe my very life to her. She was brilliant, beautiful, and loyal to the end. I shall always treasure her memory. To you, her daughters, I pledge my friendship, forever and ever."

Hey, diddle, diddle!
The cat and the fiddle,

The cow jumped over the moon;

Hey Diddle

The little dog laughed
To see such sport,

And the dish ran away
with the spoon.

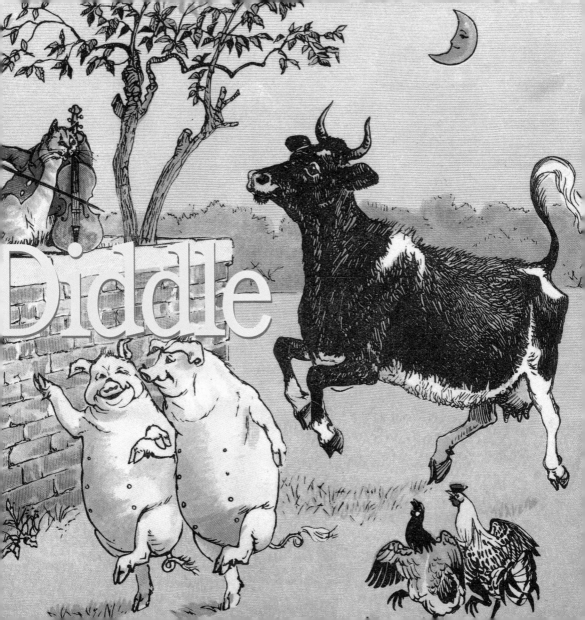

Itsy, Bitsy Spider

The itsy, bitsy spider climbed up the waterspout.

Down came the rain

And washed the spider out.

Out came the sun

And dried up all the rain.

And the itsy, bitsy spider climbed up the spout again.

"The time has come," the Walrus said, "to talk of many things: Of shoes— and ships— and sealing wax— Of cabbages— and kings . . ."

– Lewis Carroll

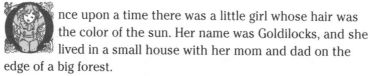

Goldilocks and the Three Bears

nce upon a time there was a little girl whose hair was the color of the sun. Her name was Goldilocks, and she lived in a small house with her mom and dad on the edge of a big forest.

One beautiful spring morning, Goldilocks went for a walk in the forest to pick some wildflowers. She wandered deeper and deeper into the woods looking for her mom's most favorite flowers, bright purple violets. Goldilocks searched long and hard, but couldn't find a single one! Finally, she started to get hungry and decided to go home. But she had walked so far, she discovered she was lost!

Goldilocks became very afraid and sat down on an old log and began to cry. Just then a bluebird flew by and let out a beautiful loud "tweet!" Startled, Goldilocks looked up and saw through her tear-filled eyes a little wooden cottage nestled between the forest trees. "Oh, thank goodness!" she cried. "I'm sure there's a grown-up living there who can help me get back home!" And she raced to the front door and banged loudly with her little fists. But nobody answered. So she walked around the house till she came to a small open window and, standing on her tippy toes, she peered inside.

This is what she saw: an empty room with a crackling fire and a long table with three steamy bowls of porridge. At the sight of the porridge, Goldilocks' stomach gave out a hungry growl. "I'll just have one or two bites while I wait for this family to come home," she thought, and climbed through the window. First she went to the largest bowl and took a heaping spoonful. "Ow!" she cried, as she put the spoon in her mouth, "this porridge is too hot!" Then she took a bite from the medium-sized bowl. "Ohhh!" she cried, "this porridge is too cold!" Finally she took a bite from the smallest bowl on the table. "Mmmm," she said, "this porridge is just right." And she ate up the whole bowl.

With a full, warm tummy, Goldilocks walked over to the glowing fire where three chairs of different sizes stood: one large, one medium, and one small. "Perhaps," she thought, "I'll have a seat here in front of the warm fire while I'm waiting." First she tried sitting in the biggest chair, but it was too high. Then she tried sitting in the middle-sized chair, but it was way too low. Finally she tried the smallest chair, and it was just right! But just as Goldilocks was curling up for a nap, the chair gave way beneath her and broke in two! Goldilocks fell to the floor and landed on

her tushy with a loud THUMP! "Ouch!" she cried, and stood up, brushing herself off.

"Maybe," she thought, "there's a nice place to sleep upstairs." So she climbed the log staircase and found herself in a large cheerful room with three beds of different sizes: one big, one medium, and one small. "How lovely it is in here," she thought. "I'll just lie down for a few minutes and rest my eyes." First she tried the largest bed, but it was too hard. Then she tried the medium-sized bed, but it was way too soft. Finally she tried the smallest bed, and it was just right. Before she knew it, Goldilocks had fallen fast asleep.

As Goldilocks dreamed upstairs of warm porridge and a crackling fire, downstairs the owners of the house returned home from their morning walk. Who lived in this little cabin tucked away in the woods? Well, three bears of course! There was big furry Papa Bear, kind pretty Mama Bear, and little fuzzy Baby Bear.

"Let's eat," said Papa Bear, "I'm starving!" As the bears took their seats at the table, Papa Bear grumbled, "Someone's been eating my porridge!" Then Mama Bear said, "Someone's been eating my porridge, too!" And then Baby Bear cried, "Someone's been eating my porridge, and there's none left for me!"

Hungry and grumpy, Papa Bear went to sit by the fire and read the morning paper. But as soon as he sat down, he growled,

"Someone's been sitting in my chair." Then Mama Bear said, "Someone's been sitting in my chair, too!" And then Baby Bear cried out, "Someone's been sitting in my chair, and they broke it in two!"

The three bears marched up the stairs to see if anything else was out of place. Papa Bear roared as he saw his bed, "Someone been sleeping in my bed!" Then Mama Bear said, "Someone's been sleeping in my bed, too!" And then Baby Bear cried, "Someone's been sleeping in my bed, and look, THERE SHE IS!!!"

Mama Bear gasped and Papa Bear let out a loud angry growl. Goldilocks woke with a terrible start. As soon as she saw the three bears towering over her she let out a piercing scream and threw herself under the covers! "Go away!" Goldilocks cried. "Go away!?" replied Baby Bear, "But we live here!"

Slowly Goldilocks peeked her head out and saw that this was just a nice normal family of bears. She explained to them how she had gotten lost looking for violets, and that she'd eaten their porridge because she was so hungry, and how the broken chair was just an accident. The bears understood and Baby Bear offered to show Goldilocks the way back to her house. She thanked them all, and asked if she could visit them again. "Of course," said Mama Bear, "if you don't get lost!" And they all laughed and hugged good-bye.

On their way back, Baby Bear showed Goldilocks a secret hidden patch of bright purple violets and Goldilocks picked a huge bunch for her mother. As they reached the edge of the forest, Goldilocks turned to say good-bye to Baby Bear, but he was already gone!

When Goldilocks got home, her parents swooped her up in their arms and kissed her cheeks, nose, and forehead. She had been gone more than two hours and they had been very worried! They were relieved to see her safe and sound at home, and her mother adored the violets!

Goldilocks told them all about her adventure with the bears and how she got back home. Her parents smiled and nodded, and praised Goldilocks for having such a wonderful imagination. At first Goldilocks tried to convince them that it wasn't make-believe, but after a while, she gave up. The three bears would have to be her own special secret.

Goldilocks never could find the bear's cottage again, no matter how hard she tried. But she did find her way back to that patch of violets, where she picked a bouquet for her mom every single week.

Mmmm . . . . Rice Pudding

This is comfort food at its finest. Rice pudding works great as a treat for your little one. For a little variety, try substituting currants or cranberries for the raisins.

2 quarts whole milk
3/4 cup long-grain rice
3 eggs
1/2 cup white sugar
1 cup whole milk
1 teaspoon vanilla extract
3/4 cup raisins
1 tablespoon
ground cinnamon

1. Pour 2 quarts milk into a large saucepan and bring to a boil over medium heat. Reduce heat to low, then mix in rice and simmer uncovered for 20 minutes, stirring frequently and skimming surface of milk as needed.
2. In a medium bowl, whisk together eggs, sugar, milk, and vanilla extract. Slowly pour into rice mixture while stirring vigorously. Allow mixture to boil and thicken, approximately 10 minutes, while stirring constantly.
3. Remove from heat and stir in raisins. Pour mixture into a 9 x 13-inch pan and sprinkle cinnamon over top. Allow to cool uncovered in refrigerator for a few hours, until pudding is chilled and firm. Cover with plastic wrap when cool.

Serves 6

Baby Feet
Edgar A. Guest

Tell me, what is half so sweet
As a baby's tiny feet,
Pink and dainty as can be,
Like a coral from the sea?
Talk of jewels strung in rows,
Gaze upon those little toes,
Fairer than a diadem,
With the mother kissing them!

It is morning and she lies
Uttering her happy cries,
While her little hands reach out
For the feet that fly about.
Then I go to her and blow
Laughter out of every toe;
Hold her high and let her place
Tiny footprints on my face.

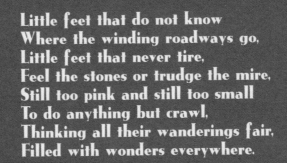

Little feet that do not know
Where the winding roadways go,
Little feet that never tire,
Feel the stones or trudge the mire,
Still too pink and still too small
To do anything but crawl,
Thinking all their wanderings fair,
Filled with wonders everywhere.

Little feet, so rich with charm,
May you never come to harm.
As I bend and proudly blow
Laughter out of every toe,
This I pray, that God above
Shall protect you with His love,
And shall guide those little feet
Safely down life's broader street.

Hush-a-B

Hush a-bye, baby,
on the tree-top!

When the wind blows
the cradle will rock;

When the bough breaks
the cradle will fall;

ye, Baby

Down will come
baby, bough,
cradle and all.

Mortal Terrors and Motherhood

Amy Herrick

Often I wonder, if it had been given to me to know beforehand what I now know about motherhood—the swift and merciless loss of innocence, how you are transformed overnight from being someone's child to being someone's parent, handed summarily a love so incandescent and irrevocable that you have to stay awake twenty-four hours a day to protect it from all the dark dangers out of left field—if I had known all this beforehand, would I have agreed to have a child?

My little one sits in his bath splashing around contentedly. I am not prepared, my breath is taken away, when suddenly he looks up and asks me point-blank if it's true that we all must die.

The answer I give him, of course, is not good news. I wait for him to say something, to rise up angrily and punch me in the nose at this, the greatest betrayal. But he just looks away and busies himself with his rubber frog.

I'm washing his face when he says, "And then after you die, you get to be a baby again?"

"Well, I don't know. Some people think after you die, you get to come back and be another person or animal."

"Do you think that?"

"No. I think after you die, you go back to nature. You become part of the trees and the grass and the sky."

"When are we going to die?"

"I don't know. I hope not for a long time. I hope I don't die until you're grown up and have your own family and children."

"What about me?"

"Oh, I don't think you're going to die till you're very old and have your own grandchildren."

"Maybe it won't happen."

"Maybe not."

I hold my breath and think about it. Who knows? Then I laugh and see how I've been duped, duped by the cunning and perfect beauty of nature's system, which used babies as a way of securing our allegiance to life, of commanding us to go forward and grow better, even though we are burdened with the certainty that in the end we must all return to dust. It is no use to ask the question would we have had them if we had known? There is no going back. We are all driven headlong by a force that has only one thing on its mind, which is to make something out of nothing, pattern out of chaos, babies out of the dust motes dancing in the void.

It is the most darling of paradoxes that as fast as the universe makes itself, it is falling apart.

One picks oneself a baby out of the pot and in an instant the world is transformed into a gigantic booby trap. You are forced to see, not only how heart-rendingly fragile a child is, but also that your own childhood is over, that there is an inevitable time limit to all things. Yet, faced with this, do you throw your hands up in despair and sink down into lassitude and indifference?

Certainly not, because here before you is that which you would jump into a burning building, or out of a speeding locomotive, for. Here before you, by a trick of light upon the bathwater, is the little stroke of genius—the face, the sign, the map—to show you your next move, to lead you through the doors of your own mortal confines to where you will outlast yourself. ❁

If the greatest

gift of all is life

then the second

must be that no

two are alike.

– Anonymous

PANCAKES

Pancakes are a reliable go-to favorite for kids when it comes to breakfast. They are easy to make anytime, but are a weekend tradition for many families. Make them extra special with a fresh fruit topping.

PANCAKES

1 1/2 cups unbleached white flour
(or cornmeal)
1 tablespoon sugar
1/4 tablespoon salt
1 tablespoon baking powder
3 eggs, separated
4 tablespoons melted butter
2 cups milk

1. Preheat the oven to 200°F.
2. In a large bowl, combine the dry ingredients.
3. In another bowl, beat the egg yolks with the melted butter and milk. Stir into the flour mixture.
4. Beat the egg whites until they form soft peaks, and gently fold them into the batter.
5. Heat a lightly buttered frying pan over medium-high heat.
6. Drop a large spoonful of batter into the pan to create each pancake. After bubbles form and start to dry on the surface of each pancake, flip it and brown it on the other side.
7. Keep the pancakes warm in the oven until ready to serve.

Serves 4 to 6

FRUIT TOPPING

1 pint raspberries, strawberries, blackberries, or blueberries
1/4 cup sugar

1. Place berries in a saucepan with three tablespoons of water and crush slightly with a spoon.
2. Cook over low heat until fruit bubbles, stirring constantly.
3. Add sugar slowly; stirring until dissolved.
4. Increase heat and bring to low boil, until it reaches desired thickness (3–10 minutes).
5. Serve warm over pancakes, or cool and store to use as jam!

The Three Little Pigs

nce upon a time there were three little pigs. Every week, mama pig gave each of the little pigs a quarter to do with as he pleased. And every week she counseled, "*Oink oink!* Put this quarter somewhere safe *oink oink!* and save it for something very important. You never know when you'll really need it *oink oink!*"

One day, shortly after the youngest pig turned eighteen, mama pig sat her sons down and said, "*Oink oink!* My dearest little pigs, you're not so very little anymore! *Oink oink!* Now that you are all grown up, it's time for you to go out into the world and make your fortune."

"But mama!" cried the youngest pig, "where shall we live?!"

"Well," replied mama pig, "you can take the money that you've saved and build yourself a little house."

"But I have almost no money left!," squealed the youngest pig, "I spent it all on yummy delicious candy!" —for he had run straight to the candy store every time he got his quarter.

"And I spent all mine on pretty new clothes!" chimed in the

The Three Little Pigs

middle pig—for he had insisted on wearing the most stylish outfits.

"I'm afraid *Oink oink!* I have no more money to give to you," said mama pig. "You'll have to get a job *oink oink!* and save up your wages."

Now, all this time, the oldest pig was very quiet. For he had saved his quarters every week just as his mama had advised, and had a nice sum of money tucked away in his piggy bank.

The three little pigs promised their mama they'd write, and off they went to seek their fortunes.

The youngest pig scraped together just enough money to build a small house made of hay and spent his days sleeping and stuffing himself with apples.

The middle pig could only afford to build a medium-sized house made of twigs and had just enough change left over to buy a sewing machine. He spent his days rolling in the mud and making himself new clothes.

The oldest pig had saved so much money, he built himself a beautiful mansion made of bricks. Every day he worked from dawn till dusk plowing and planting the fields around his house, until he was a very successful farmer.

One day, while the youngest pig was taking a nap, a big bad wolf came out of the woods and banged loudly on his door.

"Little pig, little pig, let me in!" growled the wolf as he licked his lips.

"Not by the hair on my chinny chin chin!" cried the little pig.

"Then I'll huff and I'll puff and I'll blow your house in!" barked the wolf.

"Go ahead and try!" called back the little pig.

So the wolf huffed and he puffed and he blew the straw house into a million pieces. The little pig screamed, "Oh no!" and ran next door to his middle brother's house.

"Help me!" squealed the youngest pig, "a big bad wolf is trying to eat me up and he's headed this way."

Sure enough, the wolf came knocking on the twig house door.

"Little pigs, little pigs, let me in!" growled the wolf.

"Not by the hair on our chinny chin chins!" cried out the two little pigs.

"Then I'll huff and I'll puff and I'll blow your house in!" barked the wolf.

"Go ahead and try!" called back the little pigs.

So the wolf huffed and he puffed and he blew the twig house into a million pieces. The little pigs screamed, "Oh no!" and ran next door to their oldest brother's house.

"Help us! Help us!" they cried, "a big bad wolf is trying to eat us up and he's headed this way."

The Three Little Pigs

"Have no fear," said the oldest pig, "you'll be safe here."

Not a moment later there was a knocking on the brick house door.

"Little pigs, little pigs, let me in!" growled the wolf.

"Not by the hair on our chinny chin chins!" cried out the three little pigs.

"Then I'll huff and I'll puff and I'll blow your house in!" barked the wolf.

"Go ahead and try!" called back the oldest pig.

So the wolf huffed and he puffed, but no matter how hard he tried he couldn't blow down the big brick house.

Just then the wolf spied the chimney on the roof and thought to himself, "I'll just climb through that chimney and take those little piggies by surprise."

"Oh little pigs," said the wolf in his sweetest voice, "I'm just putting my legs in your chimney. No need to be afraid."

"Go right ahead," said the youngest pig.

"Now I'm just putting my arms in the chimney," said the wolf.

"That's fine with us," chirped the middle pig.

"And I think I'll just poke my head in, too," said the wolf, who thought he was being very sly.

"Be our guest," called out the oldest pig.

The Three Little Pigs

Suddenly, the big bad wolf slid down the chimney into the little pig's house. But the surprise was on him. The three little pigs had lit a great fire in the fireplace and the wolf landed SPLAT! right in the middle of it.

"OOOHHHH! OOOOOOHH! OOOOOOOH!" howled the wolf as he leapt back out of the chimney in one big jump and went running into the forest with his tail on fire!

The three little pigs shouted out with joy, and sang:

> "Who's afraid of the big bad wolf,
> the big bad wolf, the big bad wolf?
> Who's afraid of the big bad wolf,
> tra la la la la!"

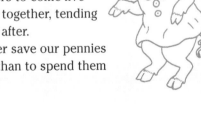

The oldest pig had so much extra room in his house that he invited his brothers to come live with him. They all went to work together, tending his farm, and lived happily ever after.

So now we see that it is better save our pennies for something really important than to spend them on silly things!

❋

Old MacDonald

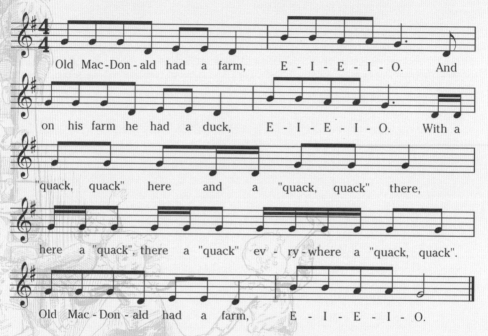

Old Mac-Don-ald had a farm, E - I - E - I - O. And
on his farm he had a duck, E - I - E - I - O. With a
"quack, quack" here and a "quack, quack" there,
here a "quack", there a "quack" ev - ry - where a "quack, quack".
Old Mac-Don - ald had a farm, E - I - E - I - O.

2. And on his farm he had some chicks, E-I-E-I-O. With a "chick, chick" here, and a "chick, chick" there. Here a "chick," there a "chick," ev'rywhere a "chick, chick." Old MacDonald had a farm, E-I-E-I-O.

3. turkey. . . "gobble, gobble"

4. pig. . . "oink, oink"

5. cow. . . "moo, moo"

6. horse. . ."neigh, neigh"

One, two,
Buckle my shoe;

Three, four,
Knock at the door;

Five, six,
Pick up sticks;

Seven, eight,
Lay them straight;

Nine, ten,
A good, fat hen;

One,
Buckle

Eleven, twelve,
Dig and delve;

Thirteen, fourteen,
Maids a-courting;

Fifteen, sixteen,
Maids in the kitchen;

Seventeen, eighteen,
Maids a-waiting;

Nineteen, twenty,
My plate's empty.

Two,
My Shoe

Adventures of Isabel
Ogden Nash

Isabel met an enormous bear;
Isabel, Isabel, didn't care.
The bear was hungry, the bear was ravenous,
The bear's big mouth was cruel and cavernous.
The bear said, Isabel, glad to meet you,
How do, Isabel, now I'll eat you!
Isabel, Isabel, didn't worry,
Isabel didn't scream or scurry.
She washed her hands and she straightened her hair up.
Then Isabel quietly ate the bear up.

Once on a night as black as pitch
Isabel met a wicked old witch.
The witch's face was cross and wrinkled,
The witch's gums with teeth were sprinkled.
Ho, ho, Isabel! the old witch crowed,
I'll turn you into an ugly toad!
Isabel, Isabel, didn't worry,
Isabel didn't scream or scurry.
She showed no rage and she showed no rancor,
But she turned the witch into milk and drank her.

Isabel met a hideous giant,
Isabel continued self-reliant.
The giant was hairy, the giant was horrid,
He had one eye in the middle of his forehead.
Good morning, Isabel, the giant said,
I'll grind your bones to make my bread.
Isabel, Isabel, didn't worry,
Isabel didn't scream or scurry.
She nibbled the zwieback that she always fed off,
And when it was gone, she cut the giant's head off.

Isabel met a troublesome doctor,
He punched and he poked till he really shocked her.
The doctor's talk was of coughs and chills
And the doctor's satchel bulged with pills.
The doctor said unto Isabel,
Swallow this, it will make you well.
Isabel, Isabel, didn't worry,
Isabel didn't scream or scurry.
She took those pills from the pill-concocter,
And Isabel calmly cured the doctor.

A Dangerous Thing to Hope For

Gail Greiner

Now, the day before Nikolai's first birthday, I not only feel guilt about those moments in the delivery room when I hung back, suspended in limbo, as if I were deciding whether or not to keep him. I feel guilt about all the times I am withdrawn from him. Being with my baby, really being present with him, is something I have to actively give myself over to. It still doesn't come naturally. Nikolai seems particularly demanding now, crawling into things he shouldn't, forever asking to be entertained. Exhausted, I get into this "my turn, your turn" thing with Michael, in an effort to get away from Nikolai. Part of my need to escape comes, I know, from my own expectation that I should be totally present, that I should stimulate Nikolai constantly, and that I should always enjoy it. Trying to make up for what I fear I lack, my presence alone isn't enough: I have to be an *uber* mother.

"When you roll a ball to him, does he roll it back?" my pediatrician asked me at a recent checkup, and I had to say I don't roll a ball to him. My cousin has taught her baby how to clap and how to throw away an acorn she's plucked up from the lawn rather than putting it in her mouth. Another cousin knows just where Nikolai is ticklish and makes him laugh a laugh

I've never heard, never elicited. My friend says "Give mummy a kiss" to her nine-month-old and her baby happily obliges, leaning forward and putting my friend's nose in her mouth. The same friend hands my own son a toy, stopping his crying instantly while I futilely bounced his seat, pleading, "Baby, baby . . ." At times like these I feel like I'm a bad mother, like I'm missing something other women were born with, some secret knowledge of how to be with a baby. Instead of simply rolling the ball, or asking for a kiss, or teaching my baby to clap, I worry that there is some magic mothering formula that I am not privy to. I forget that Nikolai and I have our own routines and rituals, that we polka around the house, play peek-a-boo and the kissing monster, that I made up new words to "Twinkle, Twinkle, Little Star" just for him. I forget that when I'm

nursing him to sleep, my hand holding his foot as he softly strokes my chest, I am with him entirely.

So now when I find myself pulling back, afraid that my happy family will somehow be snatched from me, I remember these things, and I remember Nikolai, so capable, so full of life, so generous in his love. He embodies life and connection, and I'm learning through him. For if there's any formula for being a good mother, it's to let my child unfold, and to be there with him when he does.

Nikolai is standing on his own for the first time today. As I watch him and clap wildly, I am filled with that mixture of happiness and sadness peculiar to mothers. Almost a year into motherhood, I have come to revel in this strange concoction. Because as I clap, tears streaming down my face, I see that it is this clapping, these tears, that are the weight and measure of my love.

✿

Twinkle, Twinkle Little Star

STRAWBERRY ICE CREAM PIE

L*et's face it, there's nothing more comforting than ice cream, even if you eat it with a spoon straight out of the container. But with just a little bit of an effort, this is a great alternative.*

For the crust:
- 1 1/2 cups finely crushed Oreo cookie crumbs
- 3 tablespoons unsalted butter, melted

For the filling:
- 2 cups strawberry ice cream, softened
- 2 cups vanilla ice cream, softened
- 16 large marshmallows
- 16 ounces frozen strawberries, thawed, with juice
- 1 cup heavy cream
- 1/4 cup sugar

1. Mix the cookie crumbs and butter until well blended. Press the crumbs firmly into a 10-inch pie plate and place in the freezer for 30 minutes.
2. Fill the bottom of the piecrust with strawberry ice cream. Freeze until firm (about 30 minutes).
3. Add a layer of vanilla ice cream on top of the strawberry layer. Freeze again until firm (about 30 minutes).
4. In a saucepan, combine the marshmallows with 2 to 3 tablespoons of juice from the strawberries. Stir over medium heat until melted. (Alternatively, you can coat the marshmallows with juice from the strawberries in a microwavable bowl and microwave on high for about 1 1/2 minutes, or until melted.) Cool.
5. Fold the strawberries into the cooled marshmallows. Spread the mixture onto the pie over the ice cream. Freeze again until firm.
6. To serve, whip the cream and sugar together until stiff. Spoon onto the pie and serve immediately.

Serves 8 to 10

The world is so full of

a number of things

I'm sure we should all be

as happy as kings.

— Robert Louis Stevenson

Bubbles

Big bubbles, small bubbles, round bubbles, long bubbles, bubbles you blow through a pipe, and bubbles you drag like a kite: all are possible with this easy-to-make bubble solution and blowers! Blow bubbles after the rain for longer-lasting bubbles.

BUBBLE SOLUTION

1/2 cup corn syrup
2 cups liquid dishwashing soap
5 cups warm water
spoon or whisk
large bowl

1. Pour the liquid ingredients into the bowl and stir until they froth and bubbles start to form.

BUBBLE BLOWERS

plastic-coated wire coat hangers or chicken wire, pliers

1. Twist one end of the wire into a small loop.
2. Trim sharp edges with pliers.
3. Dip loop into bubble solution and blow.

tin can, can opener, pliers

1. Remove both ends of a clean can with can opener.
2. Trim sharp edges with pliers.
3. Dip can into bubble solution and drag through the air.

paper orange juice or milk carton, scissors, tape, straw

1. Cut out one side of carton.
2. Cut out a circle about 5 inches in diameter from the piece of carton.
3. Cut circle in half, roll into a cone, and tape edges of cone together.
5. Make a hole near the tip of the cone.
6. Insert a straw into the hole and secure in place with tape.
7. Pour a bit of bubble solution into cone and blow through straw.

BANANA BREAD

This is the ultimate healthy snack for little ones. It can substitute for cookies, or be served with fruit or yogurt for breakfast or dessert.

8 tablespoons (1 stick) unsalted butter, softened, plus 1 tablespoon for greasing the pan
2 cups all-purpose flour
1 tablespoon baking powder
$1/4$ teaspoon salt
1 cup packed brown sugar
1 teaspoon grated lemon rind
2 eggs
2 cups mashed bananas (about 4 or 5 very ripe bananas)
1 cup chopped walnuts
$1/4$ teaspoon ground nutmeg
$1/2$ teaspoon vanilla extract
$1/2$ teaspoon ground cinnamon

1. Preheat the oven to 350°F. Grease a 9 x 5 x 3-inch pan with 1 tablespoon of the butter.
2. In a large bowl, mix together the flour, baking powder, and salt.
3. In a separate bowl, blend the remaining butter, sugar, and lemon rind until smooth. Beat in the eggs, and then add the flour mixture.
4. Mix in the bananas, walnuts, nutmeg, and vanilla.
5. Pour the batter into the prepared pan and sprinkle with the cinnamon.
6. Bake for 1 hour. Check to see if the sides have pulled away from the pan; if not, bake for another 10 minutes.
7. Let bread cool in pan for ten minutes before removing it.

Makes 1 loaf

The Princess and the Pea

Once upon a time there was a handsome Prince who lived in a big stone castle with his father and mother, the King and Queen. He had everything a young man could want: wealth, good looks, and all the sweets he could eat! And yet, the Prince was very sad. He wandered around the castle halls day and night, leaving behind him a fresh trail of tear drops.

The King and Queen were very worried about their son. One evening, they begged him to explain what was wrong.

"You have everything a young man could want. What could be causing you such despair?" pleaded his mother.

"I have everything but the one thing I most long for: True love. I wish to have a princess at my side and a family of my own," said the Prince.

The King and Queen agreed it was finally time for their son to marry. But there were no princesses left in all the kingdom for their dear Prince to woo. So they decided to send him on a journey around the world, where he might find the princess of his dreams.

The Prince was gone for many days and many nights. He visited far away cities and towns, from China to Peru, and met many nice princesses. Some were beautiful, some were kind, some were funny, and others quite serious. But none of them captured the Prince's heart. You see, there is no formula for why two people fall in love; it's one of the greatest mysteries. But the Prince felt sure he'd know when he found the right young lady.

All gloom and doom, the Prince returned home to his mother and father, who consoled him with a hundred hugs and kisses.

Some days later, a terrible storm raged across the land, shaking the walls with booming CRACKS of thunder, and charging the sky with enormous BOLTS of lightning. As the Prince lay in his bed that night, staring hopelessly out the window, he heard a banging on the castle's front door. Wrapping himself in a blanket, he descended the long winding staircase to the entry hall. BANG! BANG! BANG! The knocking grew louder and louder. As he pulled open the heavy wooden door it let out a loud CREAK. Standing there before him was a young woman soaked from head to toe and shivering from the freezing rain. As the Prince raised his eyes to meet the girl's gaze, he fell instantly head-over-heels in love.

"Come in, dear lady, come in," said the Prince and ushered her into the front parlor, where he wrapped her in his blanket and fed her hot chocolate with extra whipped cream. The King and Queen awoke and rushed down to see what all the commotion was about.

Through chattering teeth, the young woman introduced herself as Princess Angeline. She had been traveling home from a trip with her chaperone when he was struck down by lightening and killed. Lost and alone, she wandered along the road, till she found herself at the walls of the castle. She thanked the King and Queen for their hospitality and, especially, the Prince, whom she couldn't take her eyes off of.

The Queen could see her son was smitten with this beautiful girl, but how could she be certain the girl was telling the truth about being a princess? Suddenly, she thought of a way to test the girl's honesty. She called in one of her maids and instructed her to place a single pea under a pile of ten mattresses in the guest room, where Angeline was to sleep. Then the Queen showed the young lady to her bed, and bid a her a good night's rest.

Angeline had never seen such a tall bed! But she didn't wish to offend her hosts, so she climbed to the very top and tucked herself in.

That night the Prince dreamt only of the beautiful Princess. But the Princess did not dream of anything at all. In fact, she barely slept a wink the whole night long!

The next morning, as the Princess joined the royal family for breakfast, the Queen asked her politely, "My dear, did you have a pleasant rest?"

"Madame, I do not wish to sound ungrateful, but that was the most uncomfortable bed I've ever slept in! I felt as though I were lying upon a huge jagged rock, and awoke all sore and covered with bruises."

"Ah-hah!" the Queen exclaimed, as she clapped her hands together, for she knew that this girl must be a princess if she had the sensitivity to feel the pea beneath all those mattresses.

Two weeks later, the Prince asked the Princess to marry him, and she accepted. On their wedding day, the Prince presented the Princess with a special gift, a beautiful gold necklace with an unusual sparkling ball dangling from the end of the chain. You see, it was that very same pea she'd slept on, dipped in real gold, and covered with glittering diamonds!

From that day forward, the Princess never took that necklace off. And she and her Prince lived happily ever after.

❃

Paper Hats

There is an old saying; "You can be as many people as you have hats," and indeed you can! Watch your little girl become a queen as she dons her royal crown, or your little boy become an elf in his magic elfin hat!

ROYAL CROWN

construction paper, scissors, tape, aluminum foil, glue

1. Cut a strip of construction paper about 3 inches high and long enough to wrap around child's head. (Tape two strips together if necessary.)
2. Draw a zigzag across the top of the strip and trim along the zigzag to form the points of the crown.
3. Cut out diamond and gem shapes from the aluminum foil sheet and glue them onto the crown.
4. Wrap strip around head and tape the two ends together to fit.

MAGIC ELFIN HAT

11 x 14 construction paper, scissors, glue, glitter, stapler, 2 pieces of ribbon, feather

1. Cut a large circle from a piece of construction paper. (To cut a circle, fold sheet of paper in half, then cut a semicircle from along the fold.)
2. Draw varieties of stars and moon crescents with a thin layer of glue and sprinkle with glitter.
3. Shake off excess glitter from circle and let dry.
4. Make a single straight cut from the outside to the center of the circle.
5. Roll into a cone, overlapping the straight edges and stapling them together to form a peaked hat.
6. Staple a length of ribbon onto each side of hat for tying under the chin.
7. Glue feather to top of hat.

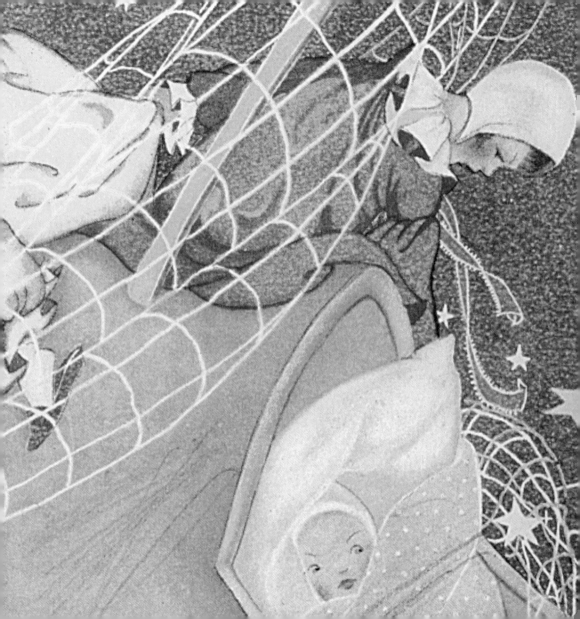

Wynken, Blynken, and Nod

Eugene Field

Wynken, Blynken, and Nod one night
    Sailed off in a wooden shoe—
Sailed on a river of crystal light,
    Into a sea of dew.
"Where are you going, and what do you wish?"
    The old moon asked the three.
"We have come to fish for the herring fish
    That live in this beautiful sea;
    Nets of silver and gold have we,"
        Said Wynken,
        Blynken,
        And Nod.

The old moon laughed and sang a song,
    As they rocked in the wooden shoe,
And the wind that sped them all night long
    Ruffled the waves of dew.
The little stars were the herring fish
    That lived in that beautiful sea;
"Now cast your nets wherever you wish,
    Never afeared are we!"
So cried the stars to the fishermen three,
        Wynken,
        Blynken,
        And Nod.

All night long their nets they threw
        To the stars in the twinkling foam;
Then down from the sky came the wooden shoe,
        Bringing the fishermen home.
'Twas all so pretty a sail, it seemed
        As if it could not be;
And some folk thought 'twas a dream they'd dreamed
        Of sailing that beautiful sea;
But I shall name you the fishermen three,
                Wynken,
                Blynken,
                And Nod.

Wynken and Blynken are two little eyes,
        And Nod is a little head,
And the wooden shoe that sailed the skies
        Is a wee one's trundle bed.
So shut your eyes while Mother sings
        Of wonderful sights that be,
And you shall see the beautiful things
        As you rock in the misty sea
Where the old shoe rocked the fishermen three,
                Wynken,
                Blynken,
                And Nod.

Pat-a-Cake

Pat-a-cake, pat-a-cake,
Baker's man!

So I do, master,
As fast as I can.

Pat it, and prick it,
And mark it with T,

Put it in the oven
For Tommy and me.

Operating Instructions

Anne Lamott

November 3

He laughed today for the first time, when Julie from upstairs was dangling her bracelets above his head while I was changing his diaper. His laughter was like little bells. Then there was the clearest silence, a hush, before total joyous pandemonium broke out between Julie and me. Then we both stared almost heartbrokenly into his face. I thought of Wallace Stevens' "Thirteen Ways of Looking at a Blackbird," verse five:

> I do not know which to prefer,
> The beauty of inflections
> Or the beauty of innuendoes,
> The blackbird whistling
> Or just after.

January 4

There are huge changes every day now. Maybe there always were, but I was too tired to notice. His main activities currently are nursing, foot sucking, making raspberries and bubbles, and chewing on his Odie doll's ear. We were sitting out beneath the moon again, nursing, and it occurred to me that someday he will stare at the full moon and know the word for it.

Things are getting better now. They've been easier for a month. People kept telling me that I just had to hold on until the end of the third month and everything would get easier. I always thought they were patronizing me or trying to keep me from scrounging up cab fare to the bridge. But I remember a month ago, when he

E.C. Pauli + Roberts.

turned three months and one or two days—it was like the baby looked at his little watch calendar and said with a bit of surprise, "Oh, for Chrissakes, it's been three months already—time to chill out a little." He sleeps every night, and doesn't cry or gritch very often, and just in general seems to be enjoying his stay a little bit more. It's much better. I'm much better. This guy I know who is really nuts and really spiritual said the other day, "My mind is a bad neighborhood that I try not to go into alone." That pretty much says it for me in the first three months.

My friend Michelle calls the first three months the fourth trimester.

Another thing I notice is that I'm much less worried all the time—a lot of things are no big deal now, whereas in the beginning everything was. For instance, now Sam can go for a few days without pooping, or can poop ten times in one day, without my automati-cally thinking he has some terrible intestinal blockage or deformity that will require a colostomy, and that will make trying to get him into day care a living hell.

He's becoming so grown-up before my very eyes. It's so painful. I want him to stay this age forever.

I look at him all the time and think, "Where'd you come from?" as if out of

the blue, some Bouvier puppy came to live here with me and the kitty. I don't really know how it happened. It seems like I was just sitting around reading a book, and what book it was I can't remember, and then all of a sudden, here he is, sucking on his foot and his Odie doll's ear.

He has this beautiful hand gesture where, when he's nursing, he reaches back with his free hand to touch and lightly pat the crown of his head, and it looks exactly like he's checking to see if his bald spot is exposed.

March 28

One thing about Sam, one thing about having a baby, is that each step of the way you simply cannot imagine loving him any more than you already do, because you are bursting with love, loving as much as you are humanly capable of—and then you do, you love him even more.

He's figuring out little concepts all the time these days, like that if something falls out of his hands, it is not instantly vaporized but just might be found somewhere on the floor. Even a week ago Sam was like some rich guy who drops some change and doesn't even give it a second glance, but now when he drops something, he slowly cranes his neck and peers downward, as if the thing fell to the floor of a canyon.

May 31

I don't remember who said this, but there really are places in the heart you don't even know exist until you love a child. Sam's been teaching me how to play again, at my ripe old age. His favorite thing right now is for me to hide a Cheerio in my mouth and then to let it peek out a tiny bit, and he goes in after it with this great frantic concentration, like it's a diamond. ✿

Open, Shut Them

Open,
Shut them.
Open,
Shut them.
Give a little clap.
Open,
Shut them.
Open,
Shut them.

Place them
in your lap.
(*Creep hands up, tickling*)
Creep them, creep them.
Creep them, creep them.
Right up to your
chin. Open wide
your little mouth,
But do not
let them in.

Where is Thumbkin?

Where is Thumbkin?
Where is Thumbkin?

Here I am!

Here I am!

How are you
today, sir?

Very well,
I thank you.

Run away,

Run away.

(Repeat with other fingers:
pointer, tall man, ring man,
baby, and all the men.)

Rub-a-dub-dub
Three men in a tub.

The butcher, the baker
And the candlestick maker.

Rub-a-Dub

Dub

Ring Around The Rosie

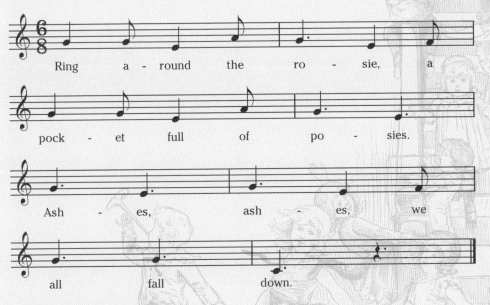

Ring a - round the ro - sie, a
pock - et full of po - sies.
Ash - es, ash - es, we
all fall down.

2. Tiptoe 'round the rosie.
   Pocket full of posies.
   Ashes, ashes, we all fall down.

3. Skip around the rosie.
   Pocket full of posies.
   Ashes, ashes, we all fall down.

4. Hop around the rosie.
   Pocket full of posies.
   Ashes, ashes, we all fall down.

5. Run around the rosie.
   Pocket full of posies.
   Ashes, ashes, we all fall down.

The Tortoise and the Hare

Once upon a time there was a tortoise (that's a land turtle!) who lived with his mom, dad, and seven older brothers. They lived in a hollow tree stump on the edge of a small pond in the midst of a great big forest. The Tortoise was especially tiny for his age and couldn't move very fast on account of his short little legs. The other kids always picked on him because they said he was such a slow poke.

Of all the animals that teased the tortoise, the hare (that's a bunny rabbit!) was the meanest. The hare would run circles around the tortoise, and say things like, "Hey, 'green bean,' is that the best you can do? I'll have hopped home and eaten ten carrots by the time you get done." The tortoise would get so mad he'd feel like bursting out of his shell, but instead he'd fix his eyes straight ahead and try to ignore the hare. But one day, the tortoise couldn't contain himself any longer. Without thinking, he blurted out to the Hare, "You're just a mean bully who picks on animals that are smaller than you. Well, I've had enough!"

"Oh yeah? What are you gonna do about it?" challenged the hare.

The Tortoise and the Hare

"I'll . . . I'll . . ." stammered the tortoise, "I'll bet that I can beat you in a footrace once around the pond. If you win I'll bring you five carrots for lunch every day for a year. But if I win, you promise to leave me alone forever and never tease me again."

The hare agreed to the bet at once. After all, he could outrun the tortoise by a mile, so how could he possibly lose?

News of the race spread throughout the forest like wildfire. Before long, a crowd of young animals had gathered around to watch. The deer and the field mice designed a finish line from small pebbles, and the fox was asked to referee.

As they were taking their places, the hare gave one more chuckle and whispered to the tortoise, "I like my carrots peeled."

Before the tortoise could respond, the fox gave a loud bark to start the race, and off they went.

Within seconds, the hare was so far ahead that the tortoise could no longer even see him. But the tortoise just kept plodding along at his own slow pace, determined to win somehow. As the hare rounded the halfway mark he looked back across the pond and saw the tortoise had made it no farther than ten feet from where they started.

"That dumb little tortoise doesn't have a chance," the hare said to himself, "he's so slow, I'll never lose! I think I'll have a little fun before I finish him off."

The Tortoise and the Hare

So the hare went back and pranced and danced around the tortoise, calling him names all the while. But the tortoise just ignored him and kept his eyes fixed straight ahead. After some time, the Hare began to get tired from all his back-flips and cartwheels.

"Perhaps I'll run ahead and find a quiet spot to catch my breath," he thought, "and then I'll end this silly race."

So the hare left the tortoise behind and settled down under a shady elm for a little rest. But before he knew it, he had fallen fast asleep.

An hour later, the tortoise passed the snoozing hare and kept on going. Just as the tortoise neared the finish line, the hare awoke and saw the tortoise about to beat him! He hopped full speed around the rest of the pond, but the tortoise was too far ahead and crossed the pebble finish line first!

"I won! I won!" cried the tortoise.

All the other animals hoisted him up in the air, cheering and calling out his name. The tortoise made a lot of new friends that day, and he never heard hide-nor-hair from that hare again.

And so it turns out that the one who is slow and steady wins out in the end!

❀

Play Dough Farm

Play dough is a childhood must, so have plenty of it on hand. Young children will appreciate the edible peanutty version while older kids will enjoy play dough for keeps to dry and paint. The small animals are fun suggestions to start with but the wonder of play dough is that the possibilities are endless.

PLAY DOUGH TO EAT

2 cups powdered milk, 2 cups smooth peanut butter, 1 cup honey, bowl, spoon

1. Combine ingredients in bowl and stir until well blended.
2. Shape, admire, and eat!

PLAY DOUGH FOR KEEPS

2 cups flour, 1 cup salt, 3/4 cup water, 2 tablespoons cooking oil, Optional: food coloring, poster paints

1. Mix flour and salt in a large bowl.
2. Add oil (and food coloring) to water. Pour water slowly into the flour mixture, kneading until it becomes soft and doughy.
3. Shape. Projects can be air-dried or dried in a 250°F oven for 1 1/2 to 2 hours and then painted.

PLAY DOUGH ANIMALS

Start with golf-ball sized play dough balls and add pieces suggested below to complete your animals.

PIG: Add two triangle ears and two small beads for eyes. Flatten a small marble-sized ball into a nose. With a toothpick, press two indents into nose for the nostrils. Finish with a curly tail.

MOUSE: Add two flattened balls for ears and two small beads for eyes. Add a ball for nose and a long thin tail. Cut off pointed ends of toothpicks and insert for whiskers.

ROOSTER: Add two small beads for eyes and two small triangles for beak. Add three smaller triangles on top for comb.

APPLE CRUMB MUFFINS

Apple picking in the fall is so much fun. A great way to use up the apples is to make applesauce, a favorite first food for little ones. Use your homemade applesauce for these delicious muffins. Any variety of apple will do. Topping is optional!

TOPPING

4 tablespoons unsalted butter, softened
$1/4$ cup flour
1 cup brown sugar
$1/2$ teaspoon cinnamon

MUFFINS

3 eggs
$1/2$ cup canola oil
1 cup applesauce
1 cup apple juice concentrate
$11/4$ cups whole wheat flour
1 cup all-purpose flour
1 tablespoon baking soda
1 teaspoon ground cinnamon
1 teaspoon ground ginger
$1/2$ teaspoon ground cloves
2 apples peeled, cored, and minced

1. Preheat oven to 350°F. Place disposable muffin cups in muffin tray and set aside.
2. Mix topping ingredients in a small bowl until sandy in texture. Set aside.
3. Beat eggs well with electric mixer, then slowly add oil, applesauce, and concentrate.
4. In a separate bowl, mix flour, baking soda, and spices. Then slowly fold into egg mixture and add apples.
5. Ladle batter into muffin cups and sprinkle crumb topping on top of each one. Bake 25–35 minutes.
6. Let cool for ten minutes.

Makes 12 to 14 muffins

APPLESAUCE

8 medium-sized apples
$3/4$ cup brown or white sugar
1 teaspoon ground cinnamon
$1/4$ cup water or apple juice

1. Peel, core, and slice apples and place in large nonstick pot with remaining ingredients.
2. Cover and cook on low heat for 30–45 minutes, stirring constantly until sauce reaches desired consistency.

Makes about 6 cups

FABULOUS FRUITS

*F*ruits are, of course, divine straight from nature, but that doesn't mean we can't bake, stuff, freeze, and dip them to our heart's content with all sorts of goodies!

BAKED APPLES STUFFED WITH GRANOLA

4 large apples (tarter varieties work best)
$2/3$ cup granola with nuts
$1/3$ cup wheat germ
2 tablespoons honey
$1/2$ cup apple juice or cider
vanilla yogurt or ice cream

1. Preheat oven to 375°F.
2. Core the apples and set them in a 9-inch pie plate.
3. Mix together granola, wheat germ, and honey. Stuff the mixture into the apple centers until full, and pile the extra on top.
4. Pour the juice in the bottom of the pan.
5. Cover with aluminum foil and bake for 1 hour and 15 minutes.
6. Serve cold with yogurt for breakfast or warm with ice cream for dessert.

Serves four

FROZEN CHOCOLATE BANANAS

6 ripe bananas, peeled and halved
1 cup semi-sweet chocolate pieces (or chocolate chips)
1 tablespoon sweet butter
1 cup walnuts, smashed (optional)

1. Insert sticks into the bananas, wrap in plastic wrap, and freeze.
2. In a double boiler over hot, but not boiling, water, melt chocolate and butter together. You can also melt in the microwave on High for 1–2 minutes.
3. Dip and roll the banana in the chocolate or swiftly spread the chocolate on with a knife.
4. To add the walnuts, roll the chocolate-dipped banana in the nuts quickly, before the chocolate hardens.
5. Eat at once or refreeze up to $1/2$ hour.

Makes 12 frozen bananas

BLENDED FRUITS

A little fresh fruit puree is a wonderful thing by itself, for a little one's dessert, or on cereal in the morning. You can puree almost any fruit in a blender (except hard fruits like apple). Add a little honey or brown sugar if the fruit is tart. Add some lemon juice to keep it from discoloring. If the blender is having a hard time, add a little more liquid. You can also increase the amount of liquid and make smoothies instead of purees. Here are four delicious combinations. Simply mix ingredients, except the toppings, in a blender 1–2 minutes until smooth. Each recipe serves 4.

BANANA-APPLE
2 bananas, cut into chunks
1 cup applesauce *(see page 51)*
1 cup plain yogurt
2 tablespoons honey (optional)
4 tablespoons wheat germ (topping)

BETTER THAN ORANGE JUICE
2 nectarines (or peaches), skinned,
    pitted, and quartered
2 cups plain yogurt
$1/2$ cup orange juice
4 tablespoons oat bran or wheat germ
1 cup crushed ice or 1 frozen
    banana (optional)
4 tablespoons raspberries (topping)

STRAWBERRY FRAPPE
1 cup fresh grapefruit or orange juice
1 cup strawberries, hulled
3 tablespoons honey (optional)
$1/2$ cup club soda
1 cup crushed ice

SUMMER HEAVEN
2 papayas, peeled, seeded, and diced
1 mango, peeled, pitted, and diced
1 cup pineapple, diced
2 bananas, peeled and cut into
    chunks
$1/4$ cup apple juice
juice from one lemon
1 cup blueberries (topping)

Little Red Riding Hood

nce upon a time there was a lovely girl who wore her favorite red hooded cape everywhere she went, even to bed! Her nickname was Little Red Riding Hood.

One sunny summer afternoon, Little Red Riding Hood's mother sent her to take a "get well" basket of chicken soup and crackers to her grandmother who had a terrible cold. Her grandmother lived near their house, in a little cabin in the woods. Little Red Riding Hood loved her grandmother more than anyone else in the whole world, except for her mother, of course.

As she set off into the forest with her basket in hand, her mother cautioned Little Red Riding Hood sternly, "Do not stray from the path even to pick berries, and no matter what, don't talk to strangers! Make sure to call me as soon as you get there!"

Little Red Riding Hood dutifully obeyed her mother's instructions and stopped only to pick berries that lined the dirt trail. About half way to her grandmother's house she stooped to pluck one especially juicy raspberry from its vine, but in so doing she tripped on a root and fell flat on the ground. The berries she

Little Red Riding Hood

had already collected scattered all over the path and her basket flipped over, spilling out everything inside.

"Oh, dear!" cried Little Red Riding Hood as she scrambled to pick up her things.

Just then, a big bad wolf jumped out from the trees where he had been watching Little Red Riding Hood for some time. He was waiting for her to walk farther into the woods so he could eat her up where no one would come upon them.

"Hello young lady," said the wicked wolf in his sweetest voice, "can I help you gather your berries?"

"Well," said Little Red Riding Hood, "you look like a nice wolf, but I'm not allowed to talk to strangers."

"I see," replied the Wolf, "then I won't say another word!" and he began picking up the berries in silence.

This seemed all right to Little Red Riding Hood. After all, her mother didn't say she couldn't gather berries with a stranger. It took some time, but finally they put all her belongings back into the basket. "My, it's getting late," yawned the big bad Wolf, "it's almost my bedtime."

Little Red Riding Hood looked at her watch and saw she had been gone almost an hour. It normally took half that time to get to her grandmother's, and her mother would surely be worried if she didn't call soon. She explained her predicament to the wolf, and he offered to show her a short cut through the woods. Now her mother had told her not to stray from the path, but the wolf seemed friendly enough, and this was a special situation, after all.

So the wolf led Little Red Riding Hood to a much smaller trail and told her to follow it straight to her grandmother's. She thanked him for his kindness and waved good-bye.

But the wolf hadn't shown her a shortcut, at all. In fact, the new path would take Little Red Riding Hood twice as long as the one she had been on. You see, when the wolf understood that she was going to visit her grandmother, he decided that a grown-up would make a much better meal than a tiny girl. He tricked Little Red Riding Hood into taking the longer way so that he could sneak ahead and eat her grandmother before she got there!

The wolf arrived at the old woman's cabin in a flash, and knocked lightly. When she called out from her bed, "Who's there?" the wicked Wolf answered in his sweetest voice, "It's just me grandma, Little Red Riding Hood."

"Well come upstairs, my dear," replied her Grandmother.

So the big bad wolf went up to the old lady's room and, before she knew it, he leapt forward and swallowed her up in one huge bite. But the Wolf was still hungry and decided to wait for Little Red Riding Hood and eat her, too, for dessert. He put on her grandmother's nightgown and sleeping cap, pulled down the

window shades, and crawled into the old woman's bed.

A few moments later, Little Red Riding Hood finally arrived. Finding her grandmother's front door wide open, she let herself in and walked right upstairs to the bedroom.

"Granny," she said, "it's me, Little Red Riding Hood. I've brought you some soup and fresh berries to make you feel better."

"Come closer where I can see you, child," called the wolf in his kindest voice, "you know how poor my vision is." So Little Red Riding Hood took a few steps forward.

"Granny, what big eyes you have," remarked Little Red Riding Hood.

"The better to see you with, dear. Now come closer," replied the sneaky wolf.

As Little Red Riding Hood took another step she said, "Granny, what big ears you have."

"The better to hear you with," explained the wolf.

"And what a big nose you have, Granny," she observed.

"The better to smell you with. Come just a little bit closer, dear," the wolf beckoned.

Little Red Riding Hood took a couple more steps till she was standing right next to the bed. "Oh Granny, what a BIG mouth you have!" she exclaimed.

"Yes," growled the Wolf, "the better to eat you with!" And with that he grabbed Little Red Riding Hood before she could run away, and swallowed her whole in one great bite.

A hunter who had been out in the woods heard Little Red Riding Hood scream in fright and followed the sound of her voice to the old lady's cabin. He ran upstairs and discovered the wolf lounging on the bed, licking his lips in post-meal satisfaction. With his big gun the hunter took aim at the wolf and shot him once, killing him instantly. Without a moment's hesitation, the hunter sliced open the wolf's belly and pulled out Little Red Riding Hood and her grandmother, who were both still alive! Little Red Riding Hood threw her arms around the hunter's neck and thanked him for saving their lives.

After Little Red Riding Hood had called her mother to tell her she was safe, she and her Grandmother invited the hunter to stay for dinner and join them for bowl of soup and berries with cream.

Little Red Riding Hood learned a very important lesson that day about listening to her mother. And you can be very sure that she NEVER left the path or talked with a stranger EVER again (especially big bad wolf strangers)!

❀

Jabberwocky
Lewis Carroll

'Twas brillig, and the slithy toves
    Did gyre and gimble in the wabe:
All mimsy were the borogoves,
    And the mome raths outgrabe.

"Beware the Jabberwock, my son!
    The jaws that bite, the claws that catch!
Beware the Jubjub bird, and shun
    The frumious Bandersnatch!"

He took his vorpal sword in hand:
    Long time the manxome foe he sought—
So rested he by the Tumtum tree,
    And stood awhile in thought.

And, as in uffish thought he stood,
    The Jabberwock, with eyes of flame,
Came whiffling through the tulgey wood,
    And burbled as it came!

One, two! One, two! And through and through
    The vorpal blade went snicker-snack!
He left it dead, and with its head
    He went galumphing back.

"And hast thou slain the Jabberwock?
    Come to my arms, my beamish boy!
O frabjous day! Callooh! Callay!"
    He chortled in his joy.

'Twas brillig, and the slithy toves
    Did gyre and gimble in the wabe:
All mimsy were the borogoves,
    And the mome raths outgrabe.

Skip to My Lou

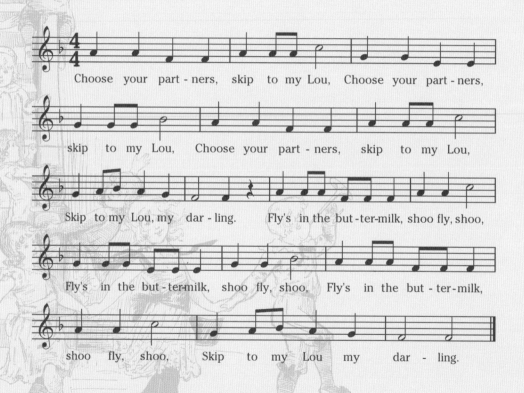

Choose your part - ners, skip to my Lou, Choose your part - ners,

skip to my Lou, Choose your part - ners, skip to my Lou,

Skip to my Lou, my dar - ling. Fly's in the but - ter-milk, shoo fly, shoo,

Fly's in the but - ter-milk, shoo fly, shoo, Fly's in the but - ter - milk,

shoo fly, shoo, Skip to my Lou my dar - ling.

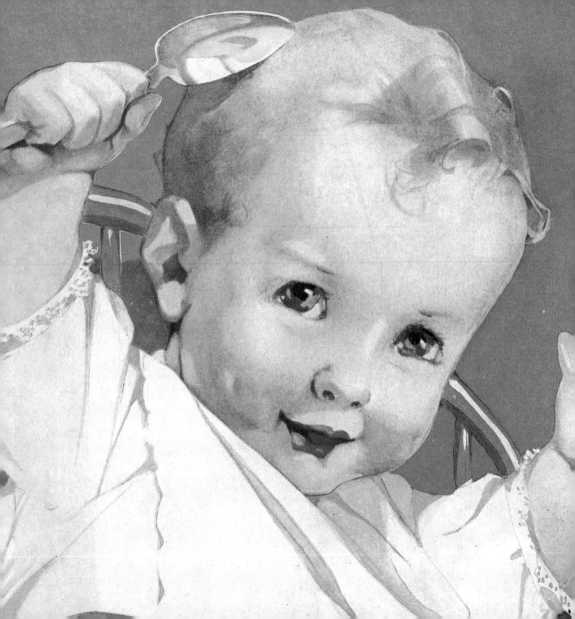

BROWNIES

These dense, fudgey brownies are a guaranteed crowd pleaser. Remember not to overcook them!

1 pound of unsalted butter
1 pound semisweet chocolate
6 extra-large eggs, beaten
2 tablespoons vanilla extract
2½ cups sugar
1½ cups flour
1 tablespoon baking powder
1 teaspoon salt
1 cup chocolate chips (semi, bitter, or milk)

1. Preheat oven to 325° F and grease a 12" x 18" pan.
2. Melt the butter and semisweet chocolate together in a double boiler over simmering water. Allow to cool slightly (do not let harden), then add eggs, vanilla, and sugar.
3. Sift dry ingredients together and add to the chocolate mixture. Then add the chocolate chips at the last minute, folding them into the batter.
4. Bake for approximately 35 to 40 minutes. Do not overcook—a toothpick WILL NOT come out clean when inserted! The center should no longer be jiggly, just slightly set. As the brownies cool, they harden and become like brownie fudge. Cool completely before cutting and serving.

Yield: 16 to 20 brownies

Valentines

Celebrate Valentine's Day by helping your child make these charming tokens of affection. The lacy doily valentine is perfect for grandparents; multiple three-dimensional valentines in miniature size are fun to hand out to little playmates; a special valentine pendant goes to that very favorite person.

LACY DOILY VALENTINE
red construction paper,
tape, glue

1. Cut 2 hearts out of red paper
2. Hinge them together with tape.
3. Glue the bottom heart onto the white doily
4. Lift the top heart to write your message.

THREE-DIMENSIONAL VALENTINE
red paper, scissors, stapler

1. Cut 4 hearts out of red paper and place on top of each other.
2. Fold hearts in half vertically to crease, and staple together down the center along the crease.

3. Spread open all the sides to make a three-dimensional heart.
4. Print a message on all 16 sides of the heart.

VALENTINE PENDANT
cardboard, red paper,
aluminum foil, glue, pink ribbon

1. Cut 3 hearts out of cardboard, red paper, and aluminum foil.
2. Holding the cardboard heart, glue red paper heart to one side and aluminum foil heart to the other.
3. Write a message on the paper side if desired.
4. Pierce a hole and loop a long pink ribbon through top of heart to make a necklace.

Five Little Monkeys

(*Bounce five fingers*)
Five little monkeys
jumping on the bed.

One fell off and
bumped his head.

Mama called the doctor,
and the doctor said,

"That's what you get

for jumping on the bed!"

*(Repeat for four, three,
two, one little monkey,
bouncing correct number
of fingers. End with "...
no more monkeys jumping
on the bed!")*

Humpty

Humpty Dumpty
sat on a wall,

Humpty Dumpty
had a great fall;

All the King's horses,
and all the King's men

Cannot put Humpty Dumpty
together again.

Dumpty

London Bridge

Lon - don Bridge is fall - ing down,

fall - ing down, fall - ing down.

Lon - don Bridge is fall - ing down,

my fair la - dy.

2. Take a key and lock her up,
lock her up, lock her up.
Take a key and lock her up,
my fair lady.

3. Build it up with iron bars,
iron bars, iron bars.
Build it up with iron bars,
my fair lady.

4. Iron bars will break and bend,
break and bend, break and bend.
Iron bars will break and bend,
my fair lady.

5. Build it up with silver and gold,
silver and gold, silver and gold.
Build it up with silver and gold,
my fair lady.

The Three Billy Goats Gruff

Once upon a time there were three billy goat brothers who lived on a grassy hillside. Vinny Gruff was the youngest and the smartest. Angelo Gruff was the middle brother, but he was neither here-nor-there. And Bubba Gruff was the oldest and the biggest, and he was what you'd call a little slow in the thinking department, which is to say, he wasn't very bright.

The three billy goats Gruff had only one thing they liked to do, and that was EAT! All day long they'd graze their hillside, stuffing their faces with thick, delicious, green grass.

One day, after a large breakfast of clovers and buttercups, the brothers Gruff looked around and discovered they had eaten up every last blade of grass on their hill. Vinny turned to his big brother, Angelo, and said, "Ya big hog! Ya went and ate all the grassiolas!" Angelo then turned to his big brother, Bubba, and said, "Hey fatso! Ya went and ate all the grassiolas! And now we ain't got no more food!" Bubba looked at his brothers with a blank stare and just said, "DUHHHH."

The Three Billy Goats Gruff

The three billy goats Gruff searched high and low for a patch of grass, but sure enough their hill was bare. Then Vinny noticed a little wooden bridge leading to another hilly pasture covered in wavy, long grass as far as the eye could see. "Even Bubba could never eat all them grassiolas!" exclaimed Vinny, and the three billy goats Gruff set off in search of the greener pasture.

Vinny led the way, but just as he reached the middle of the bridge, a big ugly troll jumped out in front of him and blocked his way. "Nobody crosses my bridge without paying a troll toll," the awful creature said.

"But I got nothin' to give ya, Mister Troll," replied Vinny in a shaky voice.

"Then I guess I'll have to eat you for dinner! And a tasty little meal you'll make, too," roared the troll.

"Well, that's just it," Vinny quickly responded, "I'm a real little guy, and not much more than skin 'n' bones. But my older brother, Angelo, should be along any moment, and he's much plumper than I am!"

"Hmmm," said the troll as he tugged at his beard, "I *am* awful hungry. All right, you may pass. I'll wait for your brother, instead."

Pretty soon Angelo arrived at the bridge, but as he tried to cross it, out jumped the troll and blocked his way. "Nobody crosses my bridge without paying a troll toll," he roared.

"But I got nothin' to give ya, Mister Troll," replied Angelo, in a voice that was neither here-nor-there.

"Then I guess I'll have to eat you for dinner. And a big delicious meal you'll make, too," roared the troll, as he licked his chops.

"It's true," said Angelo, "I would make a good dinner. But soon my older brother, Bubba, will come along and he's twice as fat as I."

"Hmmm," said the troll as he scratched on his chin," I *am* rather hungry. All right billy goat, you may pass. I'll wait for your bigger brother instead."

Not long after, Bubba wandered over to the bridge. With each step he took the wooden bridge creaked under his massive weight. Suddenly, the troll jumped out and blocked his path. "Nobody cross-es my bridge without paying a troll toll," he roared.

"Duh, what?" said Bubba.

"I said," the troll yelled louder, "nobody crosses my bridge without paying a troll toll!"

"Duh, what's a toll?" asked Bubba.

Well, the big ugly troll had had enough of Bubba's questions. By now he was so hungry his growling stomach demanded to be fed. So with wide open jaws, the troll charged at the billy goat and ran right into him at full speed.

But Bubba didn't even budge an inch. Running into Bubba was like hitting a brick wall!

Stunned and dazed, the troll backed up and fell head first into the rushing stream below. The troll gurgled and splashed in the freezing water, and as the current whisked him away down the stream, he cried out, "Help! I . . . can't . . . swimmmmm." Soon, he completely disappeared from sight.

"Duh, I'm hungry," thought Bubba, and off he went across the bridge to meet up with his brothers.

And so, the three billy goats Gruff spent the rest of their days stuffing their bellies with fresh green grass and they never saw that big ugly troll again!

Life Doesn't Frighten Me
Maya Angelou

Shadows on the wall
Noises down the hall
Life doesn't frighten me at all
Bad dogs barking loud
Big ghosts in a cloud
Life doesn't frighten me at all.
Mean old Mother Goose
Lions on the loose
They don't frighten me at all
Dragons breathing flame
On my counterpane
That doesn't frighten me at all.
I go boo
Make them shoo
I make fun
Way they run
I won't cry
So they fly
I just smile
They go wild
Life doesn't frighten me at all.
Tough guys fight

All alone at night
Life doesn't frighten me at all.
Panthers in the park
Strangers in the dark
No, they don't frighten me at all.
That new classroom where
Boys all pull my hair
(Kissy little girls
With their hair in curls)
They don't frighten me at all.
Don't show me frogs and snakes
And listen for my scream,
If I'm afraid at all
It's only in my dreams.
I've got a magic charm
That I keep up my sleeve,
I can walk the ocean floor
And never have to breathe.
Life doesn't frighten me at all
        Not at all
        Not at all.
Life doesn't frighten me at all.

Little Miss Muffet
Sat on a tuffet,
Eating of curds and whey;

There came a big spider,
And sat down beside her,

And frightened
Miss Muffet away.

Little Miss

Muffet

The Ugly Duckling

nce upon a time there was a mother duck who lived in the tall grass on the edge of a great pond. It was spring-time and she was preparing a nest for her new little eggs to hatch in. One day, as she was coming home from gathering leaves to make beds for her soon-to-be ducklings, she came across a lone egg at the foot of her nest. "Oh dear," said Mother Duck, "one of my many babies must have fallen from my nest." Although the egg looked unfamiliar to her, she figured its shape must have changed during its fall, and she picked it up in her mouth and gently placed it back with the rest of her little eggs.

The next day, the eggs began to tremble and shake and, before long, cute duckling heads started popping out of their shells. Raoul was first, and with his sharp beak and narrow eyes, Mother Duck was sure he would be the heartbreaker of the great pond. Then came Uma and Prudence with their thick yellow hair. Mother Duck knew at once they would be the envy of all their duckling girlfriends. Next came Baxter and Max who busted out of their shells with such force that Mother Duck worried they would become the bullies of the pond.

The last egg to crack was the one that Mother Duck was the most concerned about. This was the odd little egg that just didn't seem to fit in with the others. When the head of her sixth duckling, Nathan, poked out of his shell, Mother Duck gasped in disbelief. He acted like a duck, he smelled like a duck, he even quacked like a duck, but there was definitely something strange about his appearance. In fact, this was the ugliest little duckling she had ever seen! And although she loved Nathan every bit as much as her other babies, she began to worry about what would become of him in the future.

All that spring, Mother Duck taught her six little ducklings how to paddle around, dunk for delicious insects and crumbs, and build cozy nests. Although Nathan's brothers and sisters let him play with them, the other ducklings on the great pond were not so friendly. When Mother Duck took her children for a swim, they would paddle around Nathan calling out nasty names and laughing at him. "You're uglier than a fat toad," they would sneer while splashing wildly. Though his brothers, Baxter and Max, would chase all the mean ducks away, he could see in their eyes that even they were ashamed of him.

The Ugly Duckling

As summer approached, the name calling and teasing got worse, and it began to affect Mother Duck's happy feathered family. Uma and Prudence, in an effort not to be associated with their ugly duckling brother, began hanging out late with other ducks and only spent time with their family when Mother Duck would put her webfoot down. Raoul whined that the stress of his home life was giving him frizzy fur, and Max and Baxter began to gain reputations as hooligans around the great pond. Nathan could see his mother's worry and decided enough was enough. "I'm the cause of all this trouble," thought Nathan, "I'm so hideous looking it's breaking up my family." So Nathan decided to sneak away to go live on the other side of the great pond, and hide away where no one would see him and laugh.

All through the long hot summer Nathan hid in the pond's tall grass far way from his brothers and sisters. He didn't see anyone the whole time, not even a tadpole. Then, one fall day, as he paddled on his back looking up at the clouds, he heard a voice behind him say, "Hey handsome, what are you doing?"

Startled, Nathan turned around to find the most beautiful swan he had ever seen. "Are you talking to me?" asked Nathan.

"Sure I am, handsome," she said back, "my name is Sofia, what's yours?"

"My name is Nathan, but I am not handsome."

"Sure you are, sweetie, you're just about the cutest boy swan I've ever laid eyes on," replied Sofia with a smile.

"What are you talking about? I'm not a swan, I'm an ugly duck!"

"You really don't know you are a swan, honey? Swim out with me to the still water and look down at your reflection."

Sure enough, when Nathan swam out into the open pond and looked down into the calm water, he saw that over the summer he had developed into a striking swan. Nathan was overjoyed and took Sofia back to meet his family who were all happy to see him and amazed at his transformation. Mother Duck hugged Nathan close and said that whether he was a swan or a duck, she'd always love him as her son, and made him promise he'd never disappear again. Even Raoul was impressed with Nathan's fine feathers and thick white coat.

The next spring, Nathan and Sofia got married and lived happily ever after. They even had their own litter of "ugly ducklings" who all, in their own time, emerged as lovely swans.

❀

Bluebirds

Two little bluebirds sitting on a hill.

One named Jack.

The other named Jill.

Fly away, Jack.

Fly away, Jill.

Come back, Jack.

Come back, Jill.

144

Frances
Brundage

Sing a song of sixpence,
A pocket full of rye;
Four-and-twenty blackbirds
Baked in a pie!

When the pie was opened
The birds began to sing:
Was not that a dainty dish
To set before the king?

Sing a Song of Sixpence

The Animal Fair

I went to the an-i-mal fair; the birds and the beasts were there. The big ba-boon by the light of the moon, was comb-ing his au-burn hair. The mon-key, he got drunk; he sat on the el-e-phant's trunk. The el-e-phant sneezed and fell to his knees and that was the end of the monk.

150

Easter Bunny Egg

Why is there an Easter Bunny? Legend has it that a mother once hid some eggs in a henhouse for an easter egg hunt. Her children startled a bunny that had gotten into the house and thought that he had left them their treats! The Easter Bunny was thus created and is presented here as a decorated egg for your child.

pot, water, white eggs, spoon,
wax crayons, pink egg dye, bowl,
scissors, pink paper, tape

1. Fill pot with water and boil eggs for 10 to 15 minutes, then remove with spoon and let cool.
2. Decorate eggs with wax crayons by drawing two circles for eyes, an upside-down triangle for a nose, whiskers on each side, and two front teeth.
3. Prepare dye in bowl, dip egg into dye, and let dry.
4. Draw and cut out long ears from pink paper, then glue them on to the egg.
5. Cut a 4 x $1/2$-inch strip of paper and tape ends together to form ring.
6. Set bunny egg on ring to stand and leave for your child to discover.

Little Bo

Little Bo-Peep
has lost her sheep,

And can't tell
where to
find them;

Leave them alone,
and they'll come home,

Peep

And bring
their tails behind them.

maggie and milly
and molly and may
E. E. Cummings

maggie and milly and molly and may
went down to the beach(to play one day)

and maggie discovered a shell that sang
so sweetly she couldn't remember her troubles,and

milly befriended a stranded star
whose rays five languid fingers were;

and molly was chased by a horrible thing
which raced sideways while blowing bubbles:and

may came home with a smooth round stone
as small as a world and as large as alone.

For whatever we lose(like a you or a me)
it's always ourselves we find in the sea

Mother, may I go out to swim?

Yes, my darling daughter:

Hang your clothes on

a hickory limb

And don't go near the water.

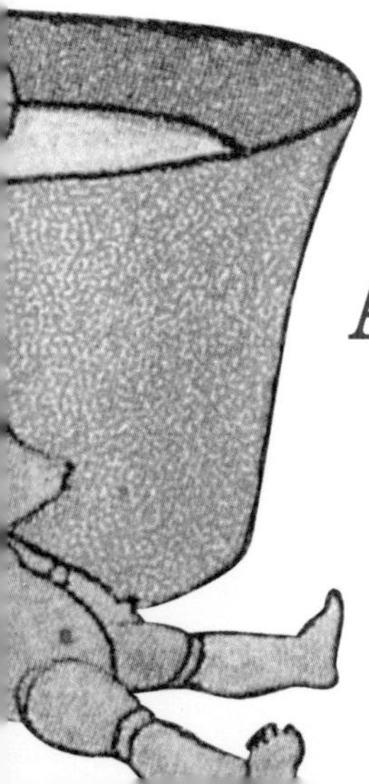

– Anonymous

It's Raining, It's Pouring

It's rain - ing, it's pour - ing, the
old man is snor - ing. He
bumped his head and fell out of bed and
could - n't get up in the morn - ing.

Rain, Rain Go Away

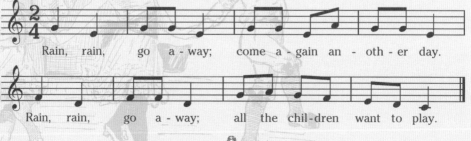

Rain, rain, go a - way; come a - gain an - oth - er day.

Rain, rain, go a - way; all the chil - dren want to play.

158

SOOTHING SOUPS

*I*s there anything more nourishing and comforting
than soup? Perfect for the tummy and the soul, soups,
especially those lovingly made and served by mom, are
sure to banish rainy- or sick-day blues.

CHICKEN VEGETABLE SOUP

3 carrots, diced
2 stalks celery, diced
2 tablespoons canola oil or butter
1 zucchini, diced
salt and pepper to taste
6 cups chicken stock
$1^{1}/_{2}$ cups dry alphabet or elbow
    pasta
2 lbs. boneless chicken breast, cut
    into small pieces
2 cups peas
$^{1}/_{2}$ cup chopped parsley (optional)
grated Parmesan cheese

1. In a skillet over medium-high heat,
   saute carrots and celery in oil for
   five minutes. Add zucchini and
   continue to cook for another 5
   minutes, stirring constantly, until
   vegetables are just slightly under-
   done. Add salt and pepper.

2. In a large soup pot, bring chicken
   stock to a boil.
3. Add pasta and cook according to
   package instructions.
4. Add cooked vegetables to pasta
   and broth.
5. Add chicken and peas and simmer
   for about 5 minutes until chicken
   is done.
6. Add parsley and adjust seasonings. Serve with cheese.

Serves 8

BROCCOLI SOUP

2 1/2 cups diced broccoli
3 cups chicken stock
2 1/2 tablespoons butter
3 tablespoons flour
3/4 cup cream
3/4 cup milk
1/4 teaspoon ground nutmeg
salt and pepper to taste

1. In a skillet over medium-high heat, cook broccoli and 1/2 cup stock until moisture is absorbed and broccoli is tender.
2. In a saucepan, melt butter over low heat, add flour and whisk into a thick paste. Add cream and milk and stir until thick.
3. Put broccoli, remaining chicken stock, nutmeg, salt and pepper in the blender and puree until smooth.
4. Add puree to cream sauce. Add more milk to thin, if desired.
5. Season and serve.

Serves 4

POTATO-LEEK SOUP

10-12 red bliss potatoes, scrubbed, or 3 baking potatoes, peeled
3 cups leeks, cleaned and chopped
4 cups chicken broth
salt and pepper to taste
1 cup milk

1. Cut potatoes into 1-inch pieces.
2. In a large soup pot, add potatoes, leeks, broth, salt and pepper. Cover and simmer about 20 minutes until the potatoes are cooked through.
3. Let cool for 10 minutes. Pour into the blender and puree until smooth.
4. Return puree to pot and add milk. Adjust seasonings and simmer on low heat for approximately 5 minutes. Add more milk to thin, if desired.

Serves 6

Sick

Shel Silverstein

"I cannot go to school today,"
Said little Peggy Ann McKay.
"I have the measles and the mumps,
A gash, a rash and purple bumps.
My mouth is wet, my throat is dry,
I'm going blind in my right eye.
My tonsils are as big as rocks,
I've counted sixteen chicken pox
And there's one more—that's seventeen,
And don't you think my face looks green?
My leg is cut, my eyes are blue—
It might be instamatic flu.
I cough and sneeze and gasp and choke,
I'm sure that my left leg is broke—
My hip hurts when I move my chin,
My belly button's caving in,
My back is wrenched, my ankle's sprained,
My 'pendix pains each time it rains.

My nose is cold, my toes are numb,
I have a sliver in my thumb.
My neck is stiff, my voice is weak,
I hardly whisper when I speak.
My tongue is filling up my mouth,
I think my hair is falling out.
My elbow's bent, my spine ain't straight,
My temperature is one-o-eight.
My brain is shrunk, I cannot hear,
There is a hold inside my ear.
I have a hangnail, and my heart is—what?
What's that? What's that you say?
You say today is . . . Saturday?
G'bye, I'm going out to play!"

Jack and Jill

Jack and Jill went up the hill,
to fetch a pail of water;

Jack fell down,
and broke his crown, and
Jill came tumbling after.

Then up Jack got and
off did trot, as fast
as he could caper,

To old Dame Dob,
who patched his nob with
vinegar and brown paper.

Jack and the Beanstalk

nce upon a time there was a young boy named Jack who lived with his mother in an old farmhouse. Jack's mother worked her fingers to the bone every day, but could not run the farm all by herself. Unfortunately, Jack was very little help. Instead of working the fields and tending the animals, he preferred dressing up as a pirate or super-hero and creating imaginary adventures around the farm. Sometimes he'd even stage military missions with secret names, like "Operation Chicken Rescue," or "Assignment: Ride the Pig."

The day finally arrived when Jack and his mother were forced to eat their very last chicken and sell their very last pig. All that remained was their old cow, Creamsicle, but even she was no longer producing milk. Jack's mother called her son into the house and said, "We have nothing left to eat or sell, except for our cow. Take her to the market and sell her for the best price you can get. We will use the money to put food on the table, until I can figure out another way to make a living."

So Jack set off on the road town with Creamsicle in tow. Not more than halfway there, Jack came upon an old peasant sitting on the side of the road.

"Hello, boy," said the old man, "what a lovely cow you have there."

"Thank you, sir," Jack replied, "I am on my way to sell her at the market."

"I would love to own such a fine animal. How much does she cost?"

Jack thought for a moment and boldly said, "Ten gold coins."

"Hmmm," said the peasant as he scratched his chin, "I have no gold coins, but I do have something even better than money." And the old man reached into his pocket and pulled out four seeds. "These bean seeds are magical and will bring the man who plants them great fortune and success. Would you like to make a trade?" asked the old man.

Ever the adventurer, Jack quickly replied, "Magic seeds! Great Fortune! You bet!" And he exchanged Creamsicle for the seeds.

Jack ran all the way home to tell his mother of his wonderful luck. Gasping for breath, he burst into the house, where his mother sat knitting by the fire. "You'll never guess what I got for the cow!" he exclaimed.

"Five gold coins?" his mother offered hopefully.

"Guess again!" replied Jack.

"Six gold coins?" asked his mother, growing more excited.

"Nope! Way better!"

"Oh Jack!" his mother gasped, "TEN GOLD COINS?"

"You're not even close," gloated Jack, and he held out his hand to show her the seeds. "I got four whole magic bean seeds."

All at once, his mother's joyful expression turned to one of terrible fury. "What have you done?!" she cried out. "How will bean seeds put food on our table?!" and she grabbed the seeds from Jack's hand and threw them out the window. Jack tried to explain that these were not ordinary seeds, but his mother would not listen to another word, and sent her son straight to bed.

The next morning, Jack awoke very early and snuck outside to collect his seeds. You can imagine his surprise when he found an enormous beanstalk growing in the exact spot where his mother had tossed the seeds just the night before. The bean stalk was as thick as the trunk of an old oak tree and reached so far into the sky that it disappeared into the clouds. Without hesitating, Jack mounted the bean stalk and climbed so high he saw birds and airplanes flying right by him!

When he finally climbed above the billowy clouds, he saw a beautiful meadow stretched out before him. At the very end of the meadow sat the most majestic castle he ever could have imagined. Cautiously, Jack stepped off the beanstalk onto the grass, and was amazed to see it was as solid as the ground below. As he started walking toward the castle, a big fat bird with shiny silver feathers swooped down and landed on top of Jack's head.

"Hello Jack!" chirped the bird.

"How do you know my name?" asked Jack with a start, for he had never heard a talking bird before!

"I know many things," the bird replied mysteriously.

"Well, if you know so much," said Jack, regaining his courage, "then tell me whose castle that is over there."

"That's easy. The castle used to belong to your father and mother, the King and Queen of Skyland," the bird explained. "But one day, a terrible giant came and killed your father. Your mother, who was pregnant with you, managed to escape to that shack down there that you call home. Then, the giant and his wife moved into the castle and took possession of everything inside it."

"That's horrible!" cried Jack, who couldn't believe his ears. "I must capture the castle back for my poor mother, and then she won't be angry with me anymore for giving away our cow! Can you help me little bird?"

"Listen to me closely," replied the bird. "You must take from the castle your father's red hen that lays golden eggs, and his self-playing harp. If you can steal these two things without being caught, you will win your kingdom back and rule the land once again. But beware! The giant has a special taste for young boys like yourself!"

But Jack was used to dangerous adventures and walked right up to the castle door and knocked loudly. Soon the giant's wife appeared. She was as tall as a skyscraper and almost as wide!

"Oh my!" said the giantess, in a voice so loud Jack nearly went deaf. "What an adorable young boy. Would you like to come inside and have a bite to eat?"

Jack agreed, and the giant's wife led him into her kitchen where she served him a huge glass of milk and a piece of cheese so big it could have fed a whole army.

As Jack ate his super-size snack the giantess told him, "I am so lonely here with my husband gone all day. Perhaps I'll keep you around for company. But you must hide as soon as my husband comes home, for he has a soft spot for the meat of young boys." No sooner had she finished talking when loud footsteps that shook the walls could be heard in the distance. "That's my husband now! Quick, into the cupboard!" Jack jumped in and, just as she shut the door behind him, the giant burst into the room. He was even bigger than his wife, and twice as ugly.

"Fee, fie, foe, fum. I smell the blood of an Englishman. Be he alive, or be he dead, I'll grind his bones to make my bread!" boomed the giant.

Jack and the Beanstalk

Jack trembled with terror while he watched through a peep-hole as the giant's eyes scanned the kitchen. But the giantess cleverly interrupted him, "Don't be silly, husband. All you smell is the delicious lamb stew I've prepared for your supper." And she brought out a large steaming bowl the size of a swimming pool and set it down on the table.

The giant slurped down his dinner in one large gulp and pushed away the empty bowl. "Bring me my red hen!" he demanded. His wife fetched him the hen and placed it in front of him.

"Hen, lay!" ordered the giant. And just like that the hen sat down and laid three golden eggs.

"Wife, bring me my harp!" barked the giant. The giantess scurried out of the kitchen and brought back the golden harp.

"Harp, play!" ordered the giant. Immediately, the harp started to play the most beautiful melody Jack had ever heard.

Before long, the giant fell fast asleep. Quietly, Jack pushed open the cabinet door and tiptoed over to the table. Picking up the hen in one arm and the harp in the other, Jack crept out of the room. But just as he reached the castle door, the harp called out, "Master! Master! A thief!"

Jack and the Beanstalk

The giant woke with a start and roared in anger as he stag-
gered to his feet. Jack hopped into high gear and sprinted across
the meadow. But the giant gained on him quickly, and by the time
Jack reached the beanstalk, the giant was only a few steps
behind. Nimble as a cat, Jack descended the vine with lightning
speed, but the giant stayed right on his heels. As Jack neared the
bottom, he could see their farmhouse and called out, "Mother,
bring me an ax!"

His mother raced from the house and handed Jack the ax just
as his feet touched the ground. Without a second to spare, Jack
whirled around and chopped down the beanstalk with one mighty
blow. As the stalk fell to the earth, the giant was crushed beneath
its enormous weight and died instantly. Moments later, the castle
in Skyland drifted gently down and settled on a grassy hillside not
far from Jack's farm.

Jack's mother wept tears of joy and held her son close.
Together they walked the path to the castle door, where Jack was
crowned King by the silver feathered bird and regained his
father's throne. Jack and his mother invited the kind giantess to
come stay in the castle, and all three of the them lived happily
ever after as one "giant" family.

❀

Mary,

Mary, Mary, quite contrary,
How does your garden grow?

Silver bells and cockle-shells,
And pretty maids all of a row.

Quite Cont

Mary,

ary

Indoor Gardening

Introduce your children to the miracle of life in plant form. The following three suggestions are easy and quick to grow. The grass and vegetable garden sprout in only a few days, almost like magic! The sweet potato plant will take about two weeks but will continue to produce a beautiful vine for your child to care for and admire.

SPONGE GRASS
sponge, water,
grass seed, saucer

1. Moisten the sponge.
2. Dip and rub the sponge in grass seed.
3. Put the sponge in a saucer of water.
4. Place the saucer in the sunlight.
5. After a few days grass should sprout on the sponge.

VEGETABLE GARDEN
root vegetables with tops
(carrots, beets, or turnips),
shallow dish, pebbles, water

1. Trim the vegetable down to the stub and leafy top.
2. Put the stub into a shallow dish of pebbles and water.

3. Keep in a sunny place and water regularly.
4. New shoots will appear in a few days.

SWEET POTATO VINE
sweet potato, toothpicks, glass jar
or large glass, water, string

1. Fill a glass just wide enough to hold potato with water.
2. Insert toothpicks around the top half of the potato.
3. Place the potato in the glass so the tip is in the water and the tooth-picks suspend the top of the potato above the top of the glass.
4. Place in a sunny window. Sprouts will appear in about two weeks.
5. As the vine starts to grow, secure some strings on the window for the vine to climb on.

Mulberry Bush

Here we go 'round the mul - ber - ry bush, the

mul - ber - ry bush, the mul - ber - ry bush.

Here we go 'round the mul - ber - ry bush, so

ear - ly in the morn - ing.

2. This is the way we wash our face,
wash our face, wash our face, so
early in the morning.

3. This is the way we comb our hair,
comb our hair, comb our hair,
so early in the morning.

4. This is the way we brush our teeth,
brush our teeth, brush our teeth,
so early in the morning.

5. This is the way we put on our
clothes, put on our clothes, put on
our clothes, so early in the morning.

The Frog Prince

nce upon a time there was a very beautiful Princess who lived with her father and three older sisters in a lovely castle. This particular Princess, however, was one of those girls who knew how pretty she was and acted quite stuck up. She often teased her sisters for not being as beautiful as she was and boasted that she, herself, was the most attractive princess in the kingdom.

One afternoon, the Princess's father became so fed up with his daughter's bragging that he forbid her from her most favorite activity: swimming in the pond behind the castle. "Until you acquire some modesty and learn to be kind to others," he chided her, "I don't want to catch even your toes in the water!"

The young Princess was so upset she ran straight to her bedroom. She banged her fists down on the bed and thought, "It's not my fault that I'm so much prettier than everyone else! Why should I be punished for saying what is true!" After she was done feeling sorry for herself, she grabbed her golden ball and went outside to sit by the edge of the pond. There she passed many hours, throwing her ball up in the air and catching it again. As evening approached, she gave the ball an extra high toss. Just as she was about to catch it, a fly bit her on the leg and she reached down to swat it, whereupon the ball sailed by her and landed with a splash in the middle of the pond and sank.

"Darn it!" exclaimed the Princess, "Now what shall I do?" She considered jumping in to retrieve it, but was too afraid of what her father would do if he caught her. "Now I've lost my favorite ball forever!" she moaned, and began to cry.

Just then, a big bullfrog jumped onto a stone beside her and croaked, "*Ribbit!* What's the matter young lady?" he asked.

"Ewww!" screamed the Princess, when she saw the frog. "You're disgusting! Go away!"

"*Ribbit!* Fine, I'll leave. I just thought *Ribbit!* I could help you get your ball back! But I see *Ribbit!* that you're a rude girl who doesn't deserve my time!" And the frog started to jump away.

Seeing him go, the Princess suddenly realized this bullfrog might be her only chance to ever see her ball again, and quickly changed her tune. "Oh, Mister Frog, please come back," she said sweetly, "I'm sorry for being so unkind. I'm just in a very grouchy mood today. I would be grateful if you could bring me my ball."

185

"Well, *Ribbit!*" replied the frog. "Perhaps if you promise to do me a favor in return *Ribbit!*"

"Anything you want," offered the Princess.

So the frog dove under the still water and returned moments later with the Princess's ball.

"Oh thank you" exclaimed the Princess. She grabbed the ball and began running back towards the castle.

"Wait!" called out the bullfrog, "you forgot my favor!"

But the Princess just kept running..

That night, while the Princess sat at the dinner table with her father and her three sisters, there was a knock on the castle door. A moment later, their butler appeared and said, "There's a frog to see the young Princess."

"Tell him to go away!" replied the Princess.

"Wait just a second," said the King, "do you know this frog, child?"

"Of course not," said the Princess, "I mean, I might have seen him once by the pond, but I would never stoop to talk to such a lowly disgusting creature."

The King eyed his daughter suspiciously. "Show the frog in. We shall see what his business is with my daughter!"

The bullfrog hopped into the Royal dining room and bowed before the King. "*Ribbit!* Your highness, I am here to collect a debt from the Princess. Today I rescued her ball from the bottom of

the pond *Ribbit!*, and she promised me a favor in return *Ribbit!*
But as soon as I returned her ball, she ran away."

"Is this true?!" boomed the King, turning to his daughter.

"I suppose I may have said something like that," grumbled the
Princess as she glared at the Frog.

"I must apologize for my selfish daughter," said the King. "Now
tell me what favor you want. I will make sure she performs it."

"Thank you, sire *Ribbit!* All I want is for the Princess to give me
a small kiss on my head *Ribbit!*"

"Yuck! I'd never kiss something that ugly!" cried the Princess.

"Silence!" shouted the King. "You will do as you promised.
Now, kiss the frog!"

"Your highness, I only wish for a kiss that is willingly given, not
forced," explained the Frog.

"Well, then, my daughter must learn to see beyond your looks.
You will stay and be the Princess's constant companion."

"Oh father, pleeeease! Don't do this to me! You're ruining my life!"

"Not one more word out of you!" commanded the King. "Now,
frog, come join us on the table."

That night, the kind frog ate from the Princess's plate, drank
from her cup and slept on her pillow. She didn't dare disobey
her father's decision, but vowed to herself never to kiss the
slimy frog as long as she lived.

The Frog Prince

The weeks passed, and slowly the Princess and the frog became inseparable. Despite her vow to hate the frog, the Princess found herself enjoying his company. He was quite a gentle, intelligent frog and had a wonderful sense of humor. The frog told her funny stories about his travels to ponds all over the world, and the Princess gave him facials and manicures. One night as they lay in bed, the Princess leaned over without thinking and kissed the frog goodnight. Suddenly, there was a clap of thunder and a puff of smoke and the frog turned into a handsome prince!

"What happened?" cried the startled Princess. "And what have you done with my dear frog!?"

"It is I, Princess," replied the Prince. "When I was a boy, a wicked witch put a curse on me, turning me into a bullfrog. Only the kiss of a princess could turn me back into my human body."

"But why didn't you tell me this weeks ago?" asked the Princess.

"Because the kiss had to come of your own free will, or it would not have worked," answered the Prince.

The Princess embraced the Prince and told him she loved him with all her heart. "Can you forgive me for taking so long to see what a beautiful person you were on the inside?" begged the Princess. And the Prince just took her head in his hands and kissed her. They were married on the Princess's eighteenth birthday, and lived happily ever after. ❀

Easy Flying Machines

Children love tossing objects into the air and are even more taken with things they can make soar and drift. Here are two easy creations to have fun with. Kids can decorate both with markers.

PAPER AIRPLANES
*rectangular piece
of thin paper*

1. Crease paper in half lengthwise, then unfold it so it lies like an open book.
2. Fold the top left corner down so that the edge of the triangular flap aligns with the center crease.
3. Do the same with the top right corner.
4. Make an additional diagonal fold on each side, aligning edges of flap to center crease.
5. Refold the main crease.
6. Turn one flap down parallel to the center crease to make a wing. Leave no more than 1 inch of space between new fold and center crease.
7. Do the same with the other flap.
8. Create the wing tips by folding and unfolding the end of each wing to form creases. The end of each wing should be slightly bent when unfolded.
9. Open both wings, hold the plane by the center flap under the wings, and throw into the air.

PARACHUTE
*4 pieces of string, handkerchief
or small square piece of cloth,
large paper clip*

1. Tie a length of string to each of the four corners of the piece of cloth.
2. Tie the loose ends of the four strings to the paper clip.
3. Ball up the handkerchief and either throw it as high into the air as possible, or drop it from a high place.
4. The parachute should pop open and drift slowly to the ground.

To market, to market,
to buy a fat pig,

Home again, home again,
jiggety jig.

To market,
to market,
to buy a fat hog,

Home again, home again,
jiggety jog.

To market, to market,
to buy a plum bun,

Home again,
home again,
market is done.

To Market

Down by the Station

Down by the sta - tion, ear - ly in the morn - ing,

see the lit - tle puf - fer bel - lies all in a row.

See the en - gine driv - er pull the lit - tle throt - tle;

chug, chug, puff, puff, off they go.

John Jacob Jingleheimer Schmidt

John   Ja - cob   Jin - gle - heim - er Schmidt,

his   name   is   my   name   too.   And   when

ev - er   I   go   out,   all   the   peo - ple shout, "There goes

John   Ja - cob Jin - gle-heim-er Schmidt!"   Dah, dah, dah, dah, dah, dah, dah.

(Repeat several times, each time softer, but loudly on the "dah, dah, dah . . .")

The Wheels on the Bus

(*Roll fists*)
The wheels on the bus
Go round and round,
Round and round,
Round and round.
The wheels on the bus
Go round and round,
All over town!

The driver on the bus
Goes "Move to the rear!
Move to the rear!
Move to the rear!"
The driver on the bus
Goes "Move to the rear!"
All over town!

(*Jump up and down*)
The people on the bus
Go up and down,
Up and down,
Up and down.
The people on the bus
Go up and down,
All over town!

The mothers on the bus
Go "Shh, shh, shh!"
"Shh, shh, shh!"
"Shh, shh, shh!"
The mothers on the bus
Go "Shh, shh, shh!"
All over town!

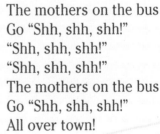

The babies on the bus
Go "Wah! Wah! Wah!"
"Wah! Wah! Wah!"
"Wah! Wah! Wah!"
The babies on the bus
Go "Wah! Wah! Wah!"
All over town!

(*Also: Wipers . . . swish;
money . . . jingle jangle;
doors . . . open and shut*)

If—
Rudyard Kipling

If you can keep your head when all about you
    Are losing theirs and blaming it on you;
If you can trust yourself when all men doubt you,
    But make allowance for their doubting too;
If you can wait and not be tired by waiting,
    Or, being lied about, don't deal in lies,
Or, being hated, don't give way to hating,
    And yet don't look too good, nor talk too wise;

If you can dream—and not make dreams your master;
    If you can think—and not make thoughts your aim;
If you can meet with triumph and disaster
    And treat those two imposters just the same;
If you can bear to hear the truth you've spoken
    Twisted by knaves to make a trap for fools,
Or watch the things you gave your life to broken,
    And stoop and build 'em up with wornout tools;

If you can make one heap of all your winnings
    And risk it on one turn of pitch-and-toss,
And lose, and start again at your beginnings
    And never breathe a word about your loss;
If you can force your heart and nerve and sinew
    To serve your turn long after they are gone,
And so hold on when there is nothing in you
    Except the Will which says to them: "Hold on";

If you can talk with crowds and keep your virtue,
    Or walk with kings—nor lose the common touch;
If neither foes nor loving friends can hurt you;
    If all men count with you, but none too much;
If you can fill the unforgiving minute
    With sixty seconds' worth of distance run—
Yours is the Earth and everything that's in it,
    And—which is more—you'll be a Man, my son!

The Old Man Who Said "Why"

E. E. Cummings

Once there was a faerie who lived on a farthest star. He was very good-natured and had yellow hair and blue eyes. Everybody in the air and everywhere and in all the stars respected him and took all their troubles to him whenever something went wrong. For millions of years he lived quietly and happily without growing any older (because he was a faerie and faeries never grow any older and he was very polite and he had a wonderful smile and a pair of golden wings.)

All the people on the stars and everywhere and in the air had wings too (although they weren't faeries themselves) because to travel in the air and everywhere and from one star to another star you have to fly. In fact, the people were flying most of the time. They would open their wings and fly down to breakfast and then fold up their wings and eat breakfast. When it was lunch time, they would fly from the air or wherever they were playing, into their houses; and fold up their wings and have a delicious luncheon made of star-petals and air-flowers. Then they'd fly upstairs and have a little nap, and when they woke up they'd fly out the window to play again away up in the air. And after supper they'd fly to bed and fall fast asleep, to dream all night about rainbows.

It wasn't very often that these people had troubles to take to the faerie; but whenever they had them, they'd fly over to the farthest star where he lived, taking their troubles with them under their arms; and he would examine all the troubles (no matter how big or how little they were, or whether they were just plain troubles or troubles in fancy boxes tied up with pink and green ribbons) and he'd give advice to all the people who brought him these troubles and would never charge them even ten cents. He liked to be nice to people, you see.

Well, after this faerie had lived happily and quietly for millions and millions of years, he woke up one morning on the farthest star and heard a murmuring all around him in the air, and this murmuring seemed to come from all the other stars. "Why what in the sky is happening?" he said to himself. All the while he was eating his breakfast, this murmuring kept getting louder and louder and louder and louder and louder and louder and louder—till finally the faerie hopped up from the table with a plate of light in one hand and a

glass of silence in the other (for he always breakfasted upon light and silence) and cried: "My gracious! Whatever is going on over there on the other stars!" He was so nervous he spilled the silence and choked on the light and then went running out very quickly on the porch. There he saw a strange sight: all the air and everywhere around his star was growing dark, and as he looked, it got darker and darker and darker and darker and darker and darker—until finally the faerie struck a match because he couldn't see. Then this darkness turned into people: he saw that the air and everywhere was dark because it was filled with millions and millions and millions and millions and millions of people. "Good Heavens!" exclaimed the faerie— "what *can* be the matter? Are all these people coming to see me and bringing their troubles? What *shall* I do?"

He was really quite scared; but he

wouldn't admit it; so he lit a candle and put on his hat and looked very wise. In a few moments the star on which he lived began to be filled with millions and millions and millions and millions of winged people who'd alighted on it. Millions and millions and millions of people began hopping and flopping and tripping and skipping and scurrying and tumbling and grumbling and hurrying toward his house. They came so fast that they almost blew out his candle: in a few seconds he found himself surrounded by millions and millions of angry neighbors, all of them carrying troubles—and the funny part of it was that these troubles all looked alike; so he knew that all the people must have the same trouble.

Before the faerie could say as much as "hello" or "how do you do" or "are you well" or "what's the matter," the millions of troubled angry people cried out together in chorus: "We want you

to help us all quickly and if you don't we'll all go mad!"

The faerie took off his hat quickly and held it before the candle—which had almost gone out because the people shouted so loudly. "But what in the air is the matter?" he cried to the millions and millions and millions and millions and millions and millions and millions of angry people.

And in one voice they all answered together: "It's the man who says 'why'!"

"Where is he?" the faerie cried, very much surprised.

"On the moon!" they all shouted, waving their troubles very fiercely.

"Well, what do you wish me to do about him?" the faerie said wisely, although he was so surprised that he didn't have a single thought in his blond head.

"You must stop him from saying 'why'!" the people screamed all together.

"Of course, of course," the faerie

promised. "Just you all go home and everything will be all right by, let me see—tomorrow morning."

"Where shall we leave our troubles?" they bellowed.

"Please to put them in the garden, under the third apple tree," the faerie said; and all the people rushed to the faerie's little garden and laid their troubles under the third apple tree which was a thousand miles tall and had red and green apples on it as big as balloons; and by the time that the last person had left his trouble, there was a pyramid of troubles around the tree right up to the apples. Then all the people politely thanked the faerie (for they were very much relieved) and they dusted their clothes and straightened their neckties and all few away.

When they had all flown away, and the farthest star was perfectly quiet again, the faerie went into his house and looked in a large book which his mother had given him, and which told him what to do. He looked under "trouble" and under "man" and under "the" and "moon" and "why," but he couldn't find a single bit of advice. "Well I never, "exclaimed this faerie. "I guess I'll have to do it all by myself!"

So, after scratching his head for five minutes, he sighed and opened his golden wings and flew out into the air and everywhere, in the direction of the moon.

He flew all night and he flew millions and millions and millions of miles; and at last (just toward morning) he saw the moon away off, looking no bigger than a penny; but as he flew toward it, it got bigger and bigger and bigger until he could see it clearly; and finally, flying very hard, he came to the very edge of the moon. And then he saw a high rock, right on the very edge of the moon, and on the top of this rock there was a tall church, and on the top of this church there was a slender steeple, and away up—right at the very top of this steeple—there was sitting a very very very very very very very old man with little green eyes and a big white beard and delicate hands like a doll's hands. And this little old man never moved and sat all by himself looking and looking and looking at nothing.

The faerie stopped flying and alighted on the moon. He folded his wings and walked up to the high rock and called to the little man, but the little man paid no attention. "That little man must be deaf," the faerie said to himself; and so he opened his wings again and flew up to the top of the rock and shouted: "Hello!" But the old old old man sitting on the steeple didn't move. "That's certainly a queer little old man," said the faerie. And so he opened his wings for the second time and flew up to the top of the church; and, standing on the roof, he cried out as loudly as ever he could to the very little old man on the steeple: "Come down!" But there was no answer and the little old man with the green eyes and the doll's hands didn't stir. "Well, I'll be wafted!" said the faerie in disgust, and so he opened his wings and flew quickly right up to the very top of the slender steeple, and alighted on it just beside the little old man; and bellowed with all his might: "What are you doing up here anyway?"

And the little very very very very very very very old man smiled, and looking at the faerie he said: "Why?"

"Because I've come all the way from the farthest star to see you," the faerie said.

"Why?" said the very very very very very very little old man.

"Just a moment and I'll tell you why," said the faerie. "I've heard a great many complaints about you—"

"Why?" said the little very very very very very old man.

"Because I've got ears, I suppose," the faerie said angrily. "Everybody in the air and everywhere and on all the stars is complaining about you and making a dreadful fuss."

"Why?" said the very very very very little old man.

"Because you say *why* all the time," said the faerie. "And it's driving everybody mad. People can't sleep and can't eat and can't think and can't fly because you're always saying why and why and why and why over and over and over again. And I've come from the farthest star to tell you that you've got to stop this why-ing."

"Why?" said the little very very very old man.

At this, the faerie grew pink with anger. "If you don't stop saying why," he said, "you'll be sorry."

"Why?" said the very very little old man.

"Now see here," the faerie said. "That's the last time I'll forgive you. Listen to me: if you say why again, you'll fall from the moon all the way to the earth."

And the little very old man smiled; and looking at the faerie, he said "why?" and he fell millions and millions and millions of deep cool new beautiful miles (and with every part of a mile he became a little younger; first he became a not very old man and next a middle-aged man and then a young man and a boy and finally a child) until, just as he gently touched the earth, he was about to be born.

❉

Old King

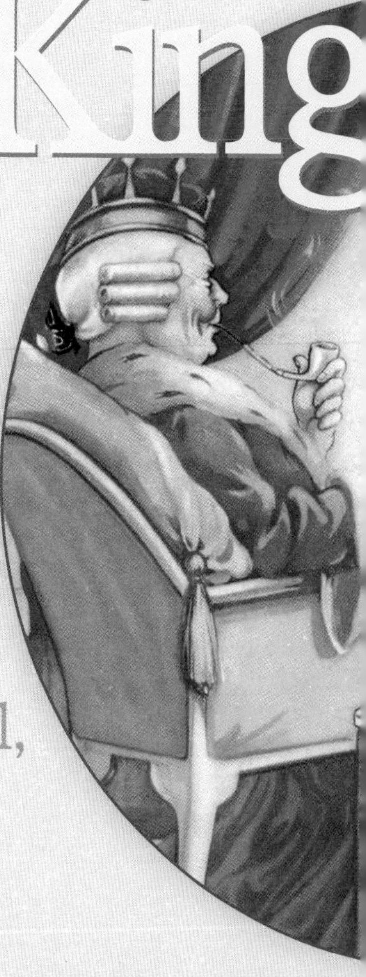

Old King Cole was a
merry old soul, and a
merry old soul was he;

He called for his pipe,
and he called for his bowl,
and he called for his
fiddlers three!

Cole

And every fiddler, he had a fine fiddle, and a very fine fiddle had he.

"Twee tweedle dee, tweedle dee" went the fiddlers.

Oh, there's none so rare as can compare with King Cole and his fiddlers three.

Homemade Music

A homemade orchestra can be quickly assembled with some basic household items. Saucepan cymbals or a spoon and overturned pot are instant noisemakers. Here are a few ideas for slightly more sophisticated instruments. Let the music begin!

WATER MUSIC
8 glasses of equal size, water, metal teaspoon

1. Line up 8 glasses side by side.
2. Fill the glass on the far left to the top with water.
3. Fill the glass 4th from the left half way.
4. Leave empty the glass farthest to the right.
5. Add water to the remaining glasses so that the level of water increases from right to left. You now have a simple scale of notes. Adjust water levels as desired to fine tune pitches.
6. Hit the glasses lightly with a metal spoon.

COMB HARMONICA
comb, tissue paper

1. Place a piece of tissue paper over a comb.
2. Blow through the tissue paper against the side of the comb.

DRUMSTICKS AND DRUM
cotton, 2 light wooden serving spoons, rubber bands, cloth, cardboard, bowl

1. Wrap cotton around wooden spoons.
2. Hold cotton in place with rubber bands.
3. Wrap cloth over cotton and secure with rubber bands.
4. Place a piece of cardboard over an open bowl.
5. Beat with serving spoon drumsticks.

Snow White and the Seven Dwarfs

nce upon a time there was a queen who was pregnant with her first child. On a frigid afternoon in the middle of winter, while the snowflakes fell heavily outside her bedroom window, the Queen gave birth to a healthy baby girl. She named her Snow White, after the color of her porcelain skin. Snow White was born with jet black hair and blood red lips, just like her mother. The Queen adored Snow White with all her soul, but on the child's one-month birthday Her Highness fell terribly ill and died shortly after. The King was left heartbroken and bereft. He did not want his daughter to grow up without a mother, however, and married again less than a year later.

The King's new wife was very vain. Her most prized possession was a magical mirror that she spoke with every morning.

"Mirror, mirror, on the wall, who's the fairest of them all?" she'd ask.

And the mirror would respond, "In all the world, I tell you 'tis true, there is no one more fair than you."

The Queen was not particularly fond of children, especially Snow White, for she was a constant reminder to the King of his beloved first wife. This was a ceaseless irritation to the Queen, and she ignored Snow White as much as possible.

As Snow White grew up, she became more and more beautiful. By the time she was sixteen, she'd become the spitting image of her mother. One morning, as the Queen finished dressing, she asked her mirror, "Mirror, mirror, on the wall, who's the fairest of them all?"

And the mirror answered, "Queen, you are very fair, 'tis true. But Snow White is ten times fairer than you."

The Queen couldn't believe what she was hearing, and flew into a rage. "This cannot be!" screamed the wicked Queen. "I refuse to stand in the shadow of a child!"

Every day for the next week, the Queen asked her mirror who was the fairest of them all, and every day it answered Snow White. By the seventh day, she had grown so angry she could barely contain herself any longer. She summoned one the King's hunters and ordered him to take Snow White deep into the woods, kill her, and bring back her heart as proof that she was dead. Though the hunter did not wish to harm Snow White, who was so kind and gentle she was adored by everyone who met her, he could not disobey his Queen.

So the hunter took Snow White far into the forest. Just as he was about to shoot her, she begged him to spare her life. "I promise not to return to the castle ever again," she pleaded, "the Queen will never know you let me free." The hunter could not help but take pity on Snow White, and he let her go. He killed a wild deer, instead, and removed its heart to give the Queen. When the hunter returned successfully, the Queen celebrated Snow White's death by feasting on her heart.

That night, Snow White wandered through the thick forest, cold and hungry, until finally the sun rose over the sky. As the morning light filtered through the trees, Snow White caught sight of an adorable cabin nestled in the woods. She knocked on the tiny door, but no one answered, so she let herself in. The first thing she saw was a long dining table set with seven extra-small plates and seven extra-small glasses. She peeked into another room and found seven extra-small beds with extra-small pillows. Without thinking, Snow White gave a huge stretch and lay down on one of the beds to rest her eyes for a moment.

The next thing she knew, Snow White awoke to find herself

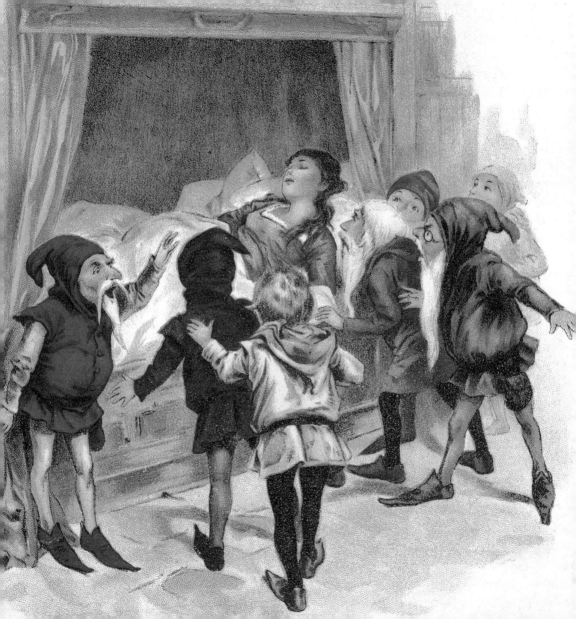

surrounded by seven friendly looking dwarfs. She heard one of them exclaim, "Look she's opening her eyes!" As she began to sit up, three of the dwarfs raced to prop her up with extra pillows.

"Who are you, miss?" asked another one of the dwarfs.

"My name is Snow White. Who are you?"

"I'm Doc," said one proudly.

"I'm Happy," piped the grinning one.

"I'm Sneezy. Ahh-chew!" said the one with the red nose.

"Bless you," said Snow White.

"I'm Sleepy. Yaaawnn . . ." said the one with droopy eyes.

"Oh, and there's Lazy sitting on the bed, Bashful under the bed, and Grumpy over by the corner," Doc added.

"How did you get here?" asked Lazy as he let out another big yawn.

Snow White told the dwarfs the story of how the Queen tried to have her killed, and asked if she could stay and live with them in exchange for doing all their cooking and cleaning. The dwarfs, who were quite smitten with Snow White's beauty and pleasant manner, immediately agreed.

Snow White and the seven dwarfs lived together happily for many weeks. Snow White missed her father dearly, but felt as though she had gained seven new brothers. She took care of their meals and laundry, and they told her silly stories for hours on end that made her laugh till her tummy ached.

In the meantime, the Queen spent her days consoling her grieving husband, who thought his daughter had run away. She hadn't bothered consulting her mirror since Snow White's death, until one morning when she happened to catch her reflection as she passed by.

"Mirror, mirror, on the wall, who's the fairest of them all?" she asked smiling.

The mirror answered, "Queen, you are very fair, 'tis true. But through the woods where the sky is bright blue, Snow White is still ten times fairer than you."

Her mirror had never lied, and the Queen felt her blood begin to boil as she realized in disgust that her stepdaughter must still be alive! That night, the Queen tossed and turned and barely slept a wink. She spent many hours concocting a plan to kill Snow White herself, and went over it a hundred times in her head until she was sure it was fail-proof.

The following morning, the Queen picked the plumpest, reddest apple she could find in their orchard and soaked it for an hour in a deadly poison. Then she dressed herself in servants' rags and smudged soot across her face. With the poison apple packed away in a basket, she set off into the forest to find Snow White. By the time she arrived at the cottage, all the dwarfs had gone off to work and Snow White was home alone. The disguised Queen tapped lightly on the door and waited. Soon a familiar voice called out, "Who is it?"

"I'm an old farmer, here to offer you some fresh-picked apples for sale," squeaked the Queen in a fake voice.

Snow White thought to herself, "I could make a delicious fresh apple pie as a treat for the dwarfs," and she opened the door.

"May I sample your wares?" Snow White asked politely. She did not recognize the evil Queen hidden beneath her peasant clothes and dirt-covered face.

"Of course," replied the Queen, and handed her the large poison apple.

"It's beautiful," remarked Snow White, as she took a big bite. She had barely even swallowed when the poison took effect, killing her in an instant. Snow White dropped to floor and the Queen clapped her hands in delight.

"You can't talk your way out of death this time!" cackled the Queen as she turned and walked away.

When the dwarfs returned home, they found the beautiful Snow White lying breathless in their doorway. They tried everything to revive her, but she was already gone. The dwarfs could not bear to bury Snow White underground where they could never look upon her lovely face again. Instead, they encased her in a glass box, which they laid next to a grave marker on the summit of a small wooded hill.

Back in the King's castle, the evil Queen asked her mirror once again, "Mirror, mirror, on the wall, who's the fairest of them all?"

The mirror replied, "In all the world, I tell you 'tis true, there is no one more fair than you." The Queen smirked with satisfaction, and went on applying her layers of make-up.

Many days passed, and the dwarfs placed new bouquets of daisies at Snow White's grave every morning. They could not help but notice that no matter how much time went by, Snow White's rosy cheeks and blood red lips never lost their vibrant color. And though she was dead, she still looked quite alive.

One summer afternoon, a prince from another kingdom was passing through the forest on horseback when he came upon Snow White lying in her glass box. He was mesmerized by her ebony hair and porcelain skin. "And those lips," he thought, "I've never seen lips that shade of crimson." He carefully took off the top of the box and lifted Snow White out, cradling her in his arms. He brushed a wisp of hair from her cheek and gently kissed her on the mouth. With a slight jolt, Snow White's eyes flew open. The Prince's kiss had brought her back to life!

When the dwarfs saw Snow White walking down the hill to their cottage, they ran outside and all embraced her at once. She hugged them back, and introduced her Prince, who proudly announced that he and Snow White were to be wed the following day.

Word spread quickly through the land that the Prince was getting married to a mysterious maiden. The Queen heard this news just as she was asking her mirror, "Mirror, mirror, on the wall, who's the fairest of them all?"

"Queen, you are very fair, 'tis true," answered the mirror, "But the Princess-to-be is ten times fairer than you."

The Queen could not believe her ears! She had to see this new rival for herself. Dressed in her most extravagant ball gown and dripping with jewels, the Queen marched into the royal church and took a seat in a front pew where she was sure to have a good view. She did not notice the seven dwarfs standing side by side in the back of the hall. As the wedding ceremony began, Snow White walked down the aisle in a beautiful dress of white beaded silk with a lace veil hiding her face. When the priest finally proclaimed the couple husband and wife, Snow White pulled back her veil to kiss the Prince. The evil Queen gasped in horror as she realized who it was and, clutching her chest, she fell dead on the spot from a heart attack.

Snow White lived happily ever after with her Prince in their great castle. They often saw Snow White's father, whose kingdom was right next to theirs. And, of course, they visited the little house in the woods and spent many fun afternoons with their special friends, the seven dwarfs.

❋

Hold Fast Your Dreams
Louise Driscoll

Hold fast your dreams!
Within your heart
Keep one, still, secret spot
Where dreams may go,
And sheltered so,
May thrive and grow—
Where doubt and fear are not.
O, keep a place apart,
Within your heart,
For little dreams to go!

Think still of lovely things that are not true.
Let wish and magic work at will in you.
Be sometimes blind to sorrow. Make believe!
Forget the calm that lies
In disillusioned eyes.
Though we all know that we must die,
Yet you and I
May walk like gods and be
Even now at home in immortality!

We see so many ugly things—
Deceits and wrongs and
  quarrelings;
We know, alas! we know
How quickly fade
The color in the west,
The bloom upon the flower,
The bloom upon the breast
And youth's blind hour.
Yet, keep within your heart
A place apart
Where little dreams may go,
May thrive and grow.
Hold fast—hold fast
  your dreams!

Mary had a little lamb,
Its fleece was white as snow;
And everywhere that Mary went
The Lamb was sure to go.

He followed her to school one day;
Which was against the rule;
It made the children laugh and play
To see a lamb at school.

And so the teacher turned him out,
But still he lingered near,
And waited patiently about
Till Mary did appear.

Mary's Lamb

Then he ran to her, and laid
His head upon her arm,
As if he said, "I'm not afraid,—
You'll keep me from all harm."

SANDWICHES & PITAS TO GO

Sandwiches are perfect for moms and kids on the go. They are quick to prepare, pack well into strollers and lunch boxes, and can be consumed with a minimal amount of mess. On these pages we have offered a range of different options, but feel free to experiment. Use cookie cutters to turn sandwiches into cool bite-sized shapes. Instead of standard white bread, use whole wheat, oatmeal, or raisin, and don't forget pita breads! They are wonderful stuffed as handy sandwiches and are the perfect size for a very easy pizza.

GRILLED CHEESE SANDWICH

2 slices rye bread
2 slices American cheese (or your
    favorite cheese)
sliced fresh tomato (optional)
slice of ham (optional)
2 tablespoons butter

1. Assemble sandwich with cheese—and tomato or ham, if desired. Heat 1 tablespoon butter in a nonstick skillet until coated.
2. Place sandwich in skillet and place something heavy on top of it (another skillet works well). Apply pressure until the downward-facing side of sandwich is golden brown.
3. Add another tablespoon of butter, flip sandwich, and repeat step 2.
4. Slice and serve warm with a big glass of milk.

SANDWICHES & PITAS TO GO

EGG SALAD SANDWICH

2 tablespoons low-fat mayonnaise
3 hard-boiled eggs (whites finely
  chopped, yolks mashed)
1/2 stalk celery, finely chopped
1/4 small Spanish onion, finely
  chopped
1/4 green pepper, finely chopped
salt and pepper to taste
6 slices sourdough bread

1. In a large bowl, mix mayonnaise and
   yolks, then add egg whites, vegetables, salt and pepper, and mix well.
2. Spoon egg salad onto bread and top
   with another piece of bread. Press
   down slightly. This is an excellent
   candidate for cookie-cutter shapes.
   The egg salad can be stored in the
   refrigerator for 2–3 days.

   Makes 3 sandwiches

STUFFED PITA

1 lb. ground beef or turkey
1 tomato, diced
1 green pepper, diced
1 onion, diced
3/4 cup bean sprouts
salt and pepper to taste
4 pita rounds, halved
shredded cheddar cheese

1. Crumble and brown meat in skillet.
2. Drain off excess fat.
3. Add tomato, pepper, onion, bean
   sprouts, salt and pepper.
4. Saute 5–10 minutes and stuff into
   pita pockets.
5. Sprinkle with cheese.

   Makes 8 small pita sandwiches

SANDWICHES & PITAS TO GO

PITA PIZZA

1 pita round
tomato sauce
broccoli or diced leftover chicken
your favorite cheeses, grated

1. Split pita into two circles.
2. Spread with tomato sauce; add
   broccoli and/or chicken and
   smother with cheeses.
3. Put on a cookie sheet and broil until
   cheese melts.

Makes two small pizzas

SANDWICH IDEAS

- Bacon, lettuce and tomato with
  mayonnaise
- Bologna and cheese
- Cheese, tomato, and sprouts
- Cold sliced hot dogs and ketchup
- Cream cheese and jelly
- Ham and cheese
- Honey and butter
- Jam and butter
- Leftover chicken with stuffing and
  cranberry sauce
- Peanut butter and jelly
- Roast beef with Russian dressing
  (or equal parts ketchup and
  mayonnaise)
- Sliced cucumber and mayonnaise
- Tuna salad with lettuce and tomato
- Turkey and lettuce with mayonnaise

Little Women

Louisa May Alcott

"Now, grandma's sixtieth birthday! Long life to her, with three times three!"

That was given with a will, as you may well believe; and the cheering once begun, it was hard to stop it. Everybody's health was proposed, from Mr. Laurence, who was considered their special patron, to the astonished guinea-pig, who had strayed from its proper sphere in search of its young master. Demi, as the oldest grandchild, then presented the queen of the day with various gifts, so numerous that they were transported to the festive scene in a wheelbarrow. Funny presents, some of them, but what would have been defects to other eyes were ornaments of grandma's,—for the children's gifts were all their own. Every stitch Daisy's patient little fingers had put into the handkerchiefs she hemmed, was better than embroidery to Mrs. March; Demi's shoe-box was a miracle of mechanical skill, though the cover

wouldn't shut; Rob's footstool had a wiggle in its uneven legs, that she declared was very soothing; and no page of the costly book Amy's child gave her, was so fair as that on which appeared, in tipsy capitals, the words,—"To dear Grandma, from her little Beth."

During this ceremony the boys had mysteriously disappeared; and, when Mrs. March had tried to thank her children, and broken down, while Teddy wiped her eyes on his pinafore, the Professor suddenly began to sing. Then, from above him, voice after voice took up the words, and from tree to tree echoed the music of the unseen choir, as

the boys sung, with all their hearts, the little song Jo had written, Laurie set to music, and the Professor trained his lads to give with the best effect. This was something altogether new, and it proved a grand success, for Mrs. March couldn't get over her surprise, and insisted on shaking hands with

every one of the featherless birds, from tall Franz and Emil to the little quadroon, who had the sweetest voice of all.

After this, the boys dispersed for a final lark, leaving Mrs. March and her daughters under the festival tree.

"I don't think I ever ought to call myself 'Unlucky Jo' again, when my greatest wish has been so beautifully gratified," said Mrs. Bhaer, taking Teddy's little fist out of the milk pitcher, in which he was rapturously churning.

"And yet your life is very different from the one you pictured so long ago. Do you remember our castles in the air?" asked Amy, smiling as she watched Laurie and John playing cricket with the boys.

"Dear fellows! It does my heart good to see them forget business, and frolic for a day," answered Jo, who now spoke in a maternal way of all mankind.

"Yes, I remember; but the life I wanted then seems selfish, lonely and cold to me now. I haven't given up the hope that I may write a good book yet, but I can wait, and I'm sure it will be all the better for such

experiences and illustrations as these;" and Jo pointed from the lively lads in the distance to her father, leaning on the Professor's arm, as they walked to and fro in the sunshine, deep in one of the conversations which both enjoyed so much, and then to her mother, sitting

enthroned among her daughters, with their children in her lap and at her feet, as if all found help and happiness in the face which never could grow old to them.

"My castle was the most nearly realized of all. I asked for splendid things to be sure, but in my heart I knew I should be satisfied, if I had a little home, and John, and some dear children like these. I've got them all, thank God, and am the happiest woman in the world;" and Meg laid her hand on her tall boy's head, with a face full of tender and devout content.

"My castle is very different from what I planned, but I would not alter it, though, like Jo, I don't relinquish all my artistic hopes, or confine myself to helping others fulfil their dreams of beauty. I've begun to model a figure of a baby, and Laurie says it is the best thing I've ever done. I think so myself, and mean to do it in marble, so that whatever happens, I may at least keep the image of my little angel."

As Amy spoke, a great tear dropped on the golden hair of the sleeping child in her arms; for her one well-beloved daughter was a frail little creature, and the dread of losing her was the shadow over Amy's sunshine. This cross was doing much for both father and mother, for one love and sorrow bound them closely together. Amy's nature was growing sweeter, deeper and more tender; Laurie was growing more serious, strong and firm, and both were learning that beauty, youth, good fortune, even love itself, cannot keep care and pain,

loss and sorrow, from the most blest; for—

*"Into each life some rain must fall,
Some days must be dark, and sad, and dreary."*

"She is growing better, I am sure of it, my dear; don't despond, but hope, and keep happy," said Mrs. March, as tender-hearted Daisy stooped from her knee, to lay her rosy cheek against her little cousin's pale one.

"I never ought to, while I have you to cheer me up, Marmee, and Laurie to take more than half of every burden," replied Amy, warmly. "He never lets me see his anxiety, but is so sweet and patient with me, so devoted to Beth, and such a stay and comfort to me always, that I can't love him enough. So, in spite of my one cross, I can say with Meg, 'Thank God, I'm a happy woman.'"

"There's no need for me to say it, for every one can see that I'm far happier than I deserve," added Jo, glancing from her good husband to her chubby children, tumbling on the grass beside her. "Fritz is getting gray and stout, I'm growing as thin as a shadow, and am over thirty; we shall never be rich, and Plumbfield may burn up any night, for that incorrigible Tommy Bangs *will* smoke sweet-fern cigars under the bedclothes, though he's set himself afire three times already. But in spite of these unro-mantic facts, I have nothing to complain of, and never was so jolly in my life. Excuse the remark, but living among boys, I can't help using their expressions now and then."

"Yes, Jo, I think your harvest will be a good one," began Mrs. March, frightening away a big black cricket, that was staring Teddy out of countenance.

"Not half so good as yours, mother. Here it is, and we never can thank you enough for the patient sowing and reaping you have done," cried Jo, with the loving impetuosity which she never could outgrow.

"I hope there will be more wheat

and fewer tares every year," said Amy softly.

"A large sheaf, but I know there's room in your heart for it, Marmee dear," added Meg's tender voice.

Touched to the heart, Mrs. March could only stretch out her arms, as if to gather children and grandchildren to herself, and say, with face and voice full of motherly love, gratitude, and humility,—

"Oh, my girls, however long you may live, I never can wish you a greater happiness than this!"

❀

Bicycle Built for Two

(Daisy, Daisy)

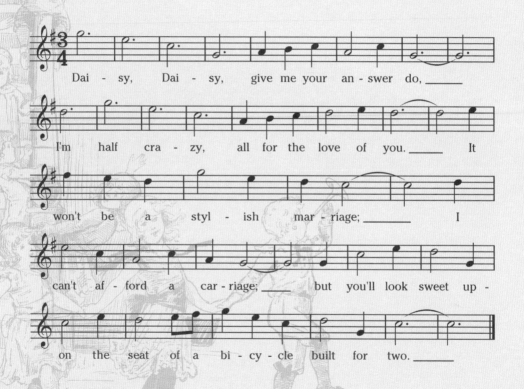

Dai - sy, Dai - sy, give me your an - swer do, _____

I'm half cra - zy, all for the love of you. _____ It

won't be a styl - ish mar - riage; _____ I

can't af - ford a car - riage; _____ but you'll look sweet up -

on the seat of a bi - cy - cle built for two. _____

Do Your Ears Hang Low?

Do you ears
hang low?

Do they wobble
to and fro?

Can you tie
them in a knot?

Can you tie
them in a bow?

Can you throw
them over your
shoulder

like a continental soldier?

Do you ears
hang low?

Head, Shoulders, Knees and Toes!

Head, shoulders, knees and toes, knees and toes!
Head, shoulders, knees and toes, knees and toes!

Eyes and ears and mouth and nose,
head, shoulders, knees and toes, knees and toes!

My Shadow
Robert Louis Stevenson

I have a little shadow that goes in and out with me,
And what can be the use of him is more than
   I can see.
He is very, very like me from the heels up
   to the head;
And I see him jump before me, when I jump
   into my bed.

The funniest thing about him is the way
   he likes to grow—
Not at all like proper children, which is
   always very slow;

For he sometimes shoots up taller like
 an India-rubber ball,
And he sometimes gets so little that
 there's none of him at all.

He hasn't got a notion of how children
 ought to play,
And can only make a fool of me in
 every sort of way.
He stays so close beside me, he's a coward
 you can see;
I'd think shame to stick to nursie as that
 shadow sticks to me!

One morning, very early, before the sun was up,
I rose and found the shining dew on
 every buttercup;
But my lazy little shadow, like an arrant sleepyhead,
Had stayed at home behind me and was
 fast asleep in bed.

Lamplight Entertainment for the Nursery

The Elephant.

The Howling Wolf.

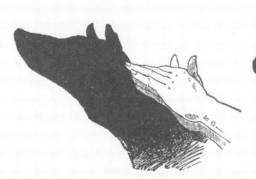

The Greyhound.

The Jockey on Horseback.

The Bird on the Wing.

The Pussycat.

The Happy Swan.

The Laughing Man.

Jack-o'-Lantern

Jack-o'-lanterns were made to frighten spirits away on Halloween—the day ghosts are believed to roam the earth. We continue this tradition today. If you can, buy a pumpkin carving kit—it will make the carving easier and safer. Do not discard the pumpkin seeds. Clean them, toss with oil and salt, and lay on a baking sheet. Bake at 350°F for 30 minutes, stirring occasionally to toast evenly. Enjoy!

large pumpkin, paring knife, spoon, pencil, paper, 2 kidney beans, 1 carrot, small candle

1. Cut around the pumpkin stem and remove top.
2. Hollow out the pumpkin with spoon.
3. Sketch out different expressions on a sheet of paper. For eyes, try triangles or half circles in different angles. For pupils, experiment with dots in different parts of the eye. Two dots on the inside corner of a triangle may suggest anger while pupils on the top curve of a half circle may suggest a happy pumpkin. For the mouth, try zig zag edges or jagged teeth.
4. Create the eyes by cutting away the outer, orange layer of the pumpkin. Do not pierce through the pumpkin flesh. For the pupils, pierce small holes through the flesh and insert the beans.
5. Create a small opening for the nose. Insert the carrot.
6. Finish with the mouth. If desired, use shallow cuts again to create the mouth shape. Then cut through the inside flesh for the teeth.
7. Place a small candle inside the pumpkin.

Peter, Peter,
pumpkin-eater,
Had a wife and
couldn't keep her;

He put her in a
pumpkin shell,
And there he kept
her very well.

The Pumpk

Cinderella

nce upon a time there was lovely little girl whose name was Cinderella. Her mother died when she was still a baby and she was raised by her father, a kind and gentle nobleman. Cinderella's father loved her so dearly he treated her like a princess. He always took her with him when he went on long trips, and he gave her beautiful dresses to wear and toys to play with. Every night he'd tell her the same bedtime story of a beautiful girl named "Cindy Rella," who grew up, fell in love with a handsome prince, and married him in a wonderful wedding ceremony at the Royal Cathedral.

When Cinderella was nine, her father remarried. His new wife was a very unfriendly woman who had two daughters of her own, named Olivia and Ingrid. The new wife was jealous of Cinderella's close relationship with her father. She also didn't like it that Cinderella was much prettier and sweeter than her two plain and grumpy daughters. In front of her husband, Cinderella's stepmother was always very nice to her, but when he wasn't around, she yelled at Cinderella all the time. Cinderella adored her father so much she could not bear to tell him how terrible her new step-mother treated her.

Two years passed, and Cinderella did her best to stay out of her stepmother's way. One day, while Cinderella splashed around in the pond behind their villa, her nasty stepsister, Olivia, came and stood by the shore. "Oh brat!" Olivia called out in her most unpleasant voice, "Mother wants to see you right away." Reluctantly, Cinderella dried off and went inside to her father's bedroom. As she opened the door, she saw her stepmother lying on the bed.

"Come here," commanded her stepmother. Cinderella walked to the bed and waited silently. "I have some bad news," she went on, "your father had an accident on the way home from his trip and fell off his horse. He struck his head on a large rock as he hit the ground, and died almost instantly."

Cinderella was stunned. She felt her knees go weak and crumpled to the floor. "How could this be?" she thought to herself, "how could there ever be a world without my father?" Cinderella could not believe that her father was gone.

"This is difficult for all of us, "continued her stepmother cold-ly, "but we must move forward with our lives. I won't allow you to roam the house weeping at all time. You may have today to grieve, but after that I wish never to hear your father's name

uttered in my home again. Do you understand?"

Cinderella nodded numbly and managed to rise to her feet. But as she left the room, her stepmother called her back and said, "I've decided to give Olivia your bedroom. I've had the maids prepare you a new room in the basement and they've already moved all your things."

From that day forward, Cinderella lived like a servant in the basement. Her stepmother took away all her fine dresses and jewelry, and Cinderella was forced to wear rags and work as a maid to her stepsisters. Without her father, there was no one left to protect her and be kind to her.

When Cinderella was sixteen, the King announced that he would host a great ball to find a bride for his son, the Prince. It had been decided that it was time for the Prince to marry, and invitations went out to all the upper-class unwed maidens in the kingdom. A royal messenger arrived with three invitations for Olivia, Ingrid, and Cinderella. Cinderella's stepmother quickly ripped up the envelope addressed to Cinderella, however, and threw it into the fire. "Maids do not go to balls!" she laughed.

Cinderella spent the next day running around sewing her sisters' ball gowns, washing their hair, applying their make-up, and helping them get ready for the party. As she waved good-bye to their carriage, she sighed to herself, "Oh how I wish I could

have gone too."

"What's with the sad face, child!" chimed a voice from behind Cinderella. The young maiden turned around and saw before her a plump old woman with apple-cheeks and the most kindly smile. She wore a long shimmery dress and held a sparkling wand in her hand.

"Who are you?" gasped Cinderella.

"Well, your fairy godmother, of course!" exclaimed the cheerful old woman. "I've come to help you get ready for your big debut!"

"What are you talking about?" asked Cinderella.

"Don't you want to go to that ball?"

"Of course, but I have nothing to wear to such a glamorous party. Look at me?!" wailed Cinderella.

"Hmmm . . . ," said the fairy godmother, "you have a point. Well, we'll just have to take care of that!" With a flourish of her wand, she turned Cinderella's rag dress into a white diamond-studded ball gown. Cinderella had diamond pins holding up ringlets in her hair and wore delicate glass slippers on her feet. Her cheeks were rosey and her mouth a pretty pink. Even her fingernails were smooth and polished. She looked like a princess!

"Oh! How beautiful!" cried Cinderella. "But how will I get to the ball? I have no carriage."

"Fetch me the largest pumpkin in your garden," answered her

fairy godmother. Cinderella ran to their yard and brought back a huge pumpkin. The old fairy waved her wand over the gourd and, with a POOF, it turned into a glittering coach made of pure gold.

"Now, check the kitchen mousetrap, and bring me as many mice as you can find," instructed her fairy godmother. When Cinderella brought back six field mice, the old woman twirled her wand again and turned them into six footmen wearing the finest velvet uniforms. Finally, the kind fairy grabbed up a rat as it scurried by and turned him into a driver for the golden carriage (that rat had the longest whiskers you've ever seen!).

As Cinderella mounted the coach, her fairy godmother warned her sternly, "You must be home by midnight, for the spell will only last till then. After that, your carriage will turn back into a pumpkin, your footmen into mice, and your gown into tattered rags."

"All right!" called back Cinderella, as her coach pulled away.

When she arrived at the ball, nobody recognized her, not even her two stepsisters, who were busy trying to attract the Prince's attention. The Prince had danced with every young maiden at the party at least twice, and complained to his father that there was no one worthy of being his bride. "Heavens to Betsy!" exclaimed the King. "There are hundreds of beautiful ladies here tonight. You are being too picky!" Just then the King noticed Cinderella standing by herself. "Look there, how about that lovely young lady?" The Prince followed his father's gaze and was love struck at the first sight of Cinderella. "Perhaps you're right, father," he mumbled as he made his way across the palace hall.

As he approached Cinderella, he bowed gracefully and asked, "My lady, may I have this dance?"

Cinderella blushed and answered with a curtsy, "I would be delighted, m'lord."

The Prince led her to the center of the floor and as the orchestra struck up a waltz, they began dancing. For the rest of the evening, they danced and talked and laughed together. The Prince was fascinated by Cinderella and paid no attention to anyone else. He did not even notice the nasty glances and jealous whispers coming from all the other maidens in the room.

"Who is that girl?" Olivia asked her sister with irritation.

"I've never seen her before! She must be from another kingdom," replied Ingrid.

"Well I wish she'd climb back under whatever rock she came

out from," pouted Olivia.

As Cinderella and the Prince shared their tenth dance, Cinderella listened in horror as the clock tower began striking midnight. Without thinking, she turned and ran from the palace, leaving the Prince standing alone in the midst of the dance floor. He called out to her, "Please! You never told me your name!" But Cinderella was already gone.

As she raced down the castle steps, she tripped and lost one of her glass slippers. She leapt into her waiting coach and reached her home just before her carriage turned back into a pumpkin, her footmen into mice, and her gown into tattered rags.

The next day, the Prince went out with his courtier to try the single glass shoe on the foot of every maiden in the kingdom. Whomever fit the slipper would have to be the young woman he had been so dazzled by the night before. Rumor spread that the shoe was a very small size, and Cinderella's stepsisters spent all morning soaking their feet in ice water to make them shrink. When the Prince and his courtier arrived at their home, both Olivia and Ingrid tried and failed to shove their big feet into the small glass slipper. Then, as the Prince was preparing to leave, Cinderella stepped forward and asked shyly, "May I try on the slipper?"

"Don't be silly," spat her stepmother, "you're just a servant girl! How could the slipper possibly belong to you?!"

"It wouldn't do any harm to let the girl try," said the courtier, kindly. "After all," he continued, "she is very pretty."

So Cinderella sat down and slipped the glass shoe onto her delicate foot.

"It's a perfect fit!" exclaimed the courtier, and he pronounced that Cinderella must be the Prince's mystery maiden.

"That's impossible!" screamed her stepmother, as she broke down in tears.

The Prince reached over and took Cinderella by the hands. Staring into her deep blue eyes, he recognized her as his true love and asked, quietly, "Will you marry me?"

She paused for a second before answering, "Yes." And the Prince embraced her in a gentle kiss.

"I was worried for a moment you might turn me down," said the Prince, as he held Cinderella close.

"How could I ever say no to my destiny?" she replied with a smile.

So the Prince and Cinderella were married in a beautiful ceremony at the Royal Cathedral, just as her father had predicted (her evil stepmother and sisters were not invited!), and lived happily ever after.

The Children's Hour
Henry Wadsworth Longfellow

Between the dark and the daylight,
    When the night is beginning to lower,
Comes a pause in the day's occupations,
    That is known as the Children's Hour.

I hear in the chamber above me
    The patter of little feet,
The sound of a door that is opened,
    And voices soft and sweet.

From my study I see in the lamplight,
    Descending the broad hall stair,
Grave Alice, and laughing Allegra,
    And Edith with golden hair.

A whisper, and then a silence:
    Yet I know by their merry eyes
They are plotting and planning together
    To take me by surprise.

A sudden rush from the stairway,
    A sudden raid from the hall!
By three doors left unguarded
    They enter my castle wall!

They climb up into my turret
    O'er the arms and back of my chair;
If I try to escape, they surround me;
    They seem to be everywhere.

They almost devour me with kisses,
    Their arms about me entwine,
Till I think of the Bishop of Bingen
    In his Mouse-Tower on the Rhine!

Do you think, O blue-eyed banditti,
    Because you have scaled the wall,
Such an old mustache as I am
    Is not a match for you all!

I have you fast in my fortress,
    And will not let you depart,
But put you down into the dungeon
    In the round-tower of my heart.

And there will I keep you forever,
    Yes, forever and a day,
Till the walls shall crumble to ruin,
    And moulder in dust away!

CHOCOLATE BIRTHDAY CUPCAKES WITH BUTTER CREAM FROSTING

*C*hocolate cupcakes children can decorate themselves at a birthday party are so much fun. You can follow this cake recipe or use your favorite dark chocolate cake mix. But do try the frosting recipe: it is the simplest, quickest, and best butter cream frosting ever! Set out a selection of frosting colors, sprinkles, m&m's, little candies, chocolate chips, etc., and let the kids be busy for hours!

CHOCOLATE CUPCAKES

4 1-ounce squares semi-sweet
    baking chocolate
1/2 cup boiling water
1 cup butter
2 cups sugar
4 eggs, separated
1 teaspoon vanilla extract
2 1/2 cups sifted cake flour
1 teaspoon baking soda
1/2 teaspoon salt
1 cup buttermilk
butter cream frosting *(recipe follows)*

1. Preheat oven to 350°F.
2. Melt chocolate in boiling water.
3. In a large bowl, cream together butter and sugar until light.
4. Add egg yolks one at a time and beat well after each addition.
5. Add vanilla and melted chocolate and mix well until blended.
6. In another bowl, mix flour, baking soda, and salt.
7. Add flour mixture alternately with buttermilk to butter and sugar mixture, beating after each addition until batter is smooth.
8. Beat egg whites until stiff and fold into cake batter.
9. Pour batter into cupcake pans lined with cupcake liners, or two round 9-inch cake pans, well buttered and dusted with dry breadcrumbs.
10. Bake 35–40 minutes until done and a toothpick inserted into the center comes out clean. Cool completely before frosting.

Makes 1 dozen cupcakes or one 2-layer cake

BUTTER CREAM FROSTING

1 lb. confectioners' sugar
$3/4$ cup butter, softened
$1^1/2$ teaspoons vanilla extract
3 tablespoons milk
food coloring (optional)
two 1-ounce squares unsweetened
   chocolate (optional)

1. In a large bowl, beat together sugar, butter, vanilla, and milk until smooth. If necessary, add more milk until frosting is a good spreading consistency.
2. If desired, divide up the frosting into different bowls and add a few drops of different food colorings to each. Stir to blend.
3. If you prefer your frosting chocolate-flavored, melt chocolate over very low heat until just melted. Stir into butter cream frosting.

Makes enough to frost 2 dozen cupcakes or to fill and frost a 2-layer cake

The Lion and the Mouse

nce upon a time there was a field mouse who lived in the forest with his wife and thirteen children. One afternoon while he was foraging for food, he came upon a large boulder covered with leaves.

"Perhaps," thought the little mouse, "I'll climb up this rock and see what food I spy with my little eye." But just as the mouse reached the top the boulder began to tremble and shake.

"An earthquake!" the mouse cried, and tried to scramble back down to the ground. Just then, a loud ROAR! came from the stone, and all the leaves that covered it flew into the air. You see, what the mouse thought was a big rock was actually a lion taking an afternoon catnap in the shade! And boy, was he angry for having been awakened so rudely!

"Why, that's no boulder!" shrieked the mouse. "That's a lion!"

The little mouse ran away as fast as his feet would carry him, but he was no match for the stealthy lion, who reached out and grabbed the mouse with one paw.

"Who dares bother the king of the jungle while he sleeps?!"

---

boomed the lion as he held the mouse right to his face.

"Oh s-s-s-ire," stuttered the mouse, "I am but a h-h-humble servant to your b-b-big b-b-bad lion self. P-p-please accept my apolog-g-gy."

"SILENCE!" roared the lion. "Now that I'm up, I'm feeling a bit hungry. You'll make the perfect snack to tide me over till suppertime." And the lion opened his massive jaws and dangled the mouse above his mouth, holding him by the tail.

"Oh, please, m-m-mister lion k-k-king of the f-forest guy," the mouse said desperately. "H-h-how's about you just let m-m-me scamper home now, and s-s-someday I'll r-r-repay the favor and s-s-save your l-l-life."

The lion started laughing so hard, he nearly dropped the mouse. "*You* save *my* life," he chuckled, "that's the funniest thing I've ever heard!"

"So whadda ya say?" continued the mouse meekly.

"Why not?" said the lion, as he wiped the tears from his eyes, "I haven't had that good a belly laugh since I can remember. You've earned your freedom. You may go." And he set the mouse down.

"Th-th-thank you, Sire!" called the mouse,

as he raced away before the lion could change his mind.

Years passed, and the mouse and his wife added ten more children to their happy family. One afternoon, while the mouse taught his youngest son how to eat a piece of swiss cheese properly, he heard a great ROAR! in the distance, which he recognized at once. He took off across the forest till he reached the lion, who lay tied up in the rope of a hunter's trap.

"Your highness," said the mouse, "are you all right?"

"Of course I'm not all right," growled the lion. "Can't you see I'm caught in this trap?"

"Perhaps I can help," offered the mouse.

The lion just snorted, "What could you possibly do, you're only a puny mouse?!"

But the mouse ignored the lion, and started to gnaw at the rope that bound him. Before long, the mouse chewed through all the ropes, setting the lion free.

The lion was so overjoyed that he gave the mouse a big lick across his face.

"YUCKK!" cried the mouse as he wiped off his entire head. "You really know how to thank a guy!"

"I owe you a big apology," said the lion.

In his coolest voice the mouse replied, "Fahgettaboutit."

The Lion and the Mouse

From that day forward, the lion and the mouse became great friends, and the mouse even asked the lion to be godfather to all his twenty-three children. So, if you ever see a lion running through the forest with a family of mice riding gleefully on his back, think of the story of the lion and the mouse, and remember that it's not the size of a person's body that matters, it's the size of their heart!

❊

Hand Puppets

Hand puppets made with brown paper bags or socks can be as simple or as decorated as age and imagination allow. A marker will suffice to draw a face on a bag or a sock for younger children. Add colored paper shapes, yarn, fabric, buttons, or dried pasta for more elaborate creations as the child grows older. (Small hard items are not for young children.) Make and collect a lot of puppets for puppet shows!

SOCK PUPPET
white tube sock, markers

1. Pull the sock over your hand as if it were your foot.
2. Thrust your thumb through the heel section and your fingers through the toe section to form a mouth.
3. Use the marker to outline a mouth.
4. Draw eyes where your knuckles are.

LION PAPER BAG PUPPET
small brown paper bag, glue, buttons, a few kernels of popped corn, 6 sticks of spaghetti, yellow yarn

1. On the flap of the bottom of a flattened paper bag, glue two buttons for eyes.
2. Glue on 3 popped kernels for a nose.
3. Glue 3 sticks of spaghetti on either side of the nose for whiskers.
4. Glue clumps of yellow yarn all around the face for a mane.

BAKED POTATOES WITH BROCCOLI & CHEESE

*E*verybody loves baked potatoes and everybody should eat lots of broccoli. This is a cozy and delicious combination. Serve it with Turkey Meatloaf Muffins (page 283) and Applesauce (page 51) for a complete meal.

4 Idaho (russet) potatoes, scrubbed and patted dry
florets from 2 small bunches broccoli
2 tablespoons butter
salt and pepper to taste
1 1/2 cups grated cheddar cheese

1. Preheat the over to 400°F.
2. Prick the potatoes all over with a fork and place on a baking sheet. Bake in middle of oven for 1 to 1 1/2 hours, until tender when pierced with a fork.
3. While potatoes are baking, steam broccoli for 3 to 5 minutes. Rinse in cold water to cool, then drain.
4. When potatoes are tender, remove baking sheet from oven, and slit potatoes open lengthwise with a fork. With oven mitts on, massage potatoes a little on all sides to make the openings wider.
5. Add butter, broccoli, salt and pepper, and sprinkle cheese on top.
6. Arrange on baking sheet and bake 10 minutes.

Serves 4

MEATBALLS & SPAGHETTI

T*his favorite combination is messy but so much fun to eat! These meatballs are so light that children call them "airballs." They are delicious straight from the frying pan but most people prefer them after they have cooked in a sauce. When leftover, slice thin and make an Italian meatball sandwich.*

1 loaf Italian bread (about 1 1/2 cups when soaked and squeezed dry)
1 lb. ground beef
1/3 cup good quality Parmesan cheese, grated
1 clove garlic, minced
4 sprigs parsley, stems removed and chopped fine
1/4 cup olive oil for frying
3 cups tomato sauce
1 lb. spaghetti

1. Cover and soak bread in water for 1/2 hour.
2. In a large bowl, mix beef, cheese, garlic, and parsley.
3. Squeeze excess water from bread and blend in a blender for a few seconds.
4. Add bread to the other ingredients and mix well with your hands.
5. Shape meatballs as round as you can, about the size of golfballs.
6. Heat the oil in a large heavy skillet until medium hot.
7. Add the meatballs gradually into the hot oil. Do not crowd the skillet.
8. Brown well on all sides and remove to paper towels to drain as they are done. The meatballs should have crisp, brown crusts on them, all the way around.
9. Simmer meatballs in tomato sauce, uncovered, for up to 3 hours.
10. Prepare spaghetti according to package instructions and serve with meatballs and sauce.

Serves 6

TURKEY SPINACH MEATLOAF

This is delicious and a great way to get spinach into your little one without much protest—they'll gobble it up! This recipe makes two loaves that will serve ten, but you can also freeze one for later.

2 lbs. lean ground turkey
2 onions, chopped and sautéed
1 bag fresh spinach, chopped fine
   (about 6 cups)
1 bunch flat-leaf parsley, chopped
   fine
1 cup bread crumbs
3 tablespoons Dijon mustard
2 large egg whites
2 teaspoons salt
1 teaspoons ground pepper
Ketchup (approximately $^1/_2$ cup)

1. Heat oven to 400°F. In a large bowl combine turkey, onions, spinach, parsley, bread crumbs, mustard, egg whites, salt, and pepper.

2. Divide mixture in half and place each half in a 9-inch loaf pan or shape into loaves on a baking sheet. Spread the top of each meatloaf with ketchup.
3. Bake until cooked through, approximately 50 minutes.

Makes 2 loaves

Rumpelstiltskin

nce upon a time there was a poor old widower who ran the town mill. His daughter, a beautiful crimson-haired maiden named Melody, worked all day alongside him. Melody had many suitors, but never paid them any attention, for she wouldn't dream of leaving her father to get married. The miller adored his daughter, and liked to tell anyone who'd listen how kind and smart she was.

One day, while the miller was fishing by a stream in the woods, the King appeared with his entourage. He was out hunting deer and looking for some fresh water to wet his parched lips. The two men struck up a conversation and, of course, the miller mentioned what a special daughter he had.

"My Melody," bragged the miller, "is so brilliant, she can do anything she sets her mind to!"

"Really," said the King, who was clearly impressed. "I heard once of a maiden so talented she could spin hay into gold. Is your daughter so brilliant that she could perform such a feat?"

"Of course she can spin hay into gold! I told you, she's brilliant and there's nothing she can't do!" the miller replied quickly, without thinking.

"Then send her to my castle tomorrow afternoon, I would like to meet this girl and see her skills with my very own eyes," replied the King, and he left the miller sitting there, wondering what he had just done.

The next day, the miller sent Melody to see the King and told her, "Just try your best. If you cannot spin the hay into gold, apologize to the King for your old father's boasting and come right home."

When Melody got to the castle the King brought her to a small room with bales of hay piled high and one spindle. "Well, young lady," smirked the King, "if you can do what your father claims, then you should have no problem spinning all this hay into gold by evening. However, if the Miller lied, and I return to find a roomful of hay, then he will be put to death for lying."

As the King left the room with a slam of the door, Melody began to whimper softly. She could not fail at this task or her father would be killed! And though she tried and tried, she could not spin even one piece of hay into gold! "What shall I do?!" she cried out to no one in particular. Just when she had all but given up and was preparing to beg for the King's mercy, a little elf appeared out of thin air. He was pale-skinned, with freckles, and white-blond hair. He wore a funny suit of purple leather, and sported a felt hat with a daisy sticking out of the rim.

"What's wrong, young lady?" asked the cheerful little man.

"Who are you?" wondered Melody suspiciously.

"Just a friend who might be able to help you out," he replied. "What seems to be the problem?"

So the miller's daughter told him her whole sad story. When she was finished, the elf thought for a moment before responding, "Well, it so happens that I am quite skilled at spinning gold from hay. But if I do this for you, what can you give me in return?"

"I have my necklace," offered Melody, "I think it's quite valuable. My father gave it to me for my sixteenth birthday."

The elf agreed, and in less than an hour he spun all the hay into beautiful threads of gold. Once he finished, the little man disappeared before Melody could even thank him.

When the King returned, he was overjoyed with the young woman's success. He gave her a bag of gold and sent her home, where she and her father celebrated their good fortune all night.

The King was greedy, however, and now that he had gotten a taste of what Melody could do, he wanted her to spin even more hay into gold. Therefore he summoned her back to the castle the following day and locked her in a bigger room, containing twice as much hay. Again he threatened her father's life if she failed, and left Melody alone to spin. The young maiden broke into tears and cried, "Help me, please! I can't let my father die!"

Just then the funny little elf appeared again and said, "Now, now, my dear, I'll help you. But have you something to give me in return?"

"I have this beautiful gold ring that belonged to my mother," and she held out her finger for the elf to see. He examined the ring closely and finally agreed. This time he took two hours to spin all the hay into gold.

When the King returned that evening, he could barely believe his eyes. He decided that he would test the maiden's ability one more time with a stable full of hay. "If you succeed this time," said the King, "I'll marry you and make you my queen."

As Melody sat in the stable surrounded by more hay than she had ever seen in her life, she lamented, "If ever I needed a miracle, it would be right now!" Suddenly, the elf appeared. "My poor little maiden," he consoled, "I am your miracle. Now tell me, what can you give me this time?"

"I have nothing left to trade," wailed Melody.

"All right," said the elf as he squinted his eyes, "if you promise to give me your firstborn child, I will spin all this hay into lovely gold."

Melody was desperate, so she agreed.

When the King came back the next morning and found all the hay turned to gold, he married Melody and she and her father moved into the castle. One year later, the new Queen gave birth to her first child, a boy. She fell instantly in love with the baby Prince and barely ever let him out of her sight.

One month later, the elf returned and demanded Melody hand over her son. She had forgotten all about her promise and begged the elf to let her keep the child, offering him all the riches in the kingdom, instead. The elf refused, though he finally took pity on the Queen, and told her that if she could guess his name within three days, he would release her from her debt. So Melody started guessing every name she had ever heard. "Tom, Henry, Douglas, Elijah?" she guessed. But to each one the elf shook his head. Then she tried some more unusual names, like "Devonshire," "Siddartha," "Usman," and "Ebeneezer." But none of them was right.

The next morning she sent all her servants out across the land to find the strangest names in the world. They returned with lengthy lists that included such bizarre names as "Bippetybop,"

"Sugarbooger," and "Scooby-Doo." She tried all of these on the elf, but he said no to each one.

On the third day, one of her courtiers returned from his search to report he had observed a peculiar little elf dancing in the forest chanting:

> "I'll feast tomorrow, I'll bake today,
> Once I take the Queen's child away!
> As soon as she loses my little game,
> I'll tell her Rumpelstiltskin is my name!"

"That's it!" cried the Queen.

When the elf arrived that afternoon, the Queen asked him, coyly, "Is your name John?"

"Nope!" replied the elf gleefully.

"How about David?"

"Uh-uh!" exclaimed the elf with a smirk.

"Hmmm," said the Queen, "could it be . . . RUMPELSTILTSKIN?!

The elf's eyes narrowed into small slits and his smile turned upside down into a frown. "How did you find out?" he screamed in shock.

"Why, it's a perfectly common name, isn't it?" replied the Queen demurely.

Rumpelstiltskin

And Rumpelstiltskin got so angry, he flew into a horrible rage. He sprang at the Queen with his fists drawn, cursing and calling her terrible names. But the Queen simply stepped aside and Rumpelstiltskin ran right into the wall behind her and was knocked out dead.

The Queen, who believed there is good in everyone, buried Rumpelstiltskin in the Royal graveyard and even gave him a large granite tombstone that read:

> "Here lies Rumpelstiltskin,
> a peach of an elf,
> who met with an early demise,
> because he cared only for himself."

Not long after, the King also passed away, and the Queen lived happily ever after in the castle with her adoring father and precious son.

✦

The Hammer Song

(Hammer fists)

Jenny works with one hammer,
one hammer, one hammer.
Jenny works with one hammer.
Then she works with two.

Jenny works with two hammers,
two hammers, two hammers.
Jenny works with two hammers.
Then she works with three.

(Stomp one foot)
Jenny works with three hammers,
three hammers, three hammers.
Jenny works with three hammers.
Then she works with four.

(Jump with both feet)

Jenny works with four hammers,
four hammers, four hammers.
Jenny works with four hammers.
Then she works with five.

(Nod head)

Jenny works with five hammers,
five hammers, five hammers.
Jenny works with five hammers . . .

Then she goes to sleep!

Potato Stamps

Play with your food: Make an assortment of potato stamps and let your kids stamp away. Flowers, hearts, stars, moons, and letters (letters need to be carved backwards) are but a few suggestions. Create designs to decorate greeting cards or wrapping paper. If you want to decorate fabric, use acrylic paint for the stamp pad.

STAMP PAD

paper towels (folded), saucers, food coloring or tempera paint

1. Make a triple layer of paper towels on top of each saucer. Use as many saucers as you want colors.
2. Check to see that paper does not hang over the edges of the dishes.
3. Thoroughly wet each pile of paper towels with different color food coloring or paint.

STAMPS

potatoes, knife

1. Cut potatoes in half.
2. Carve designs about 1/4 inch deep into flat ends of potatoes.
3. Cut away the excess pieces so you can see designs clearly.
4. Press designs into stamp pad, and stamp onto paper.

Little

Jack Horner

Little Jack Horner
Sat in the corner,
Eating of Christmas pie:

He put in his thumb,
And pulled out a plum,

And said,
"What a good boy am I!"

A Visit from St. Nicholas
Clement Clarke Moore

'Twas the night before Christmas, when all through the house
Not a creature was stirring, not even a mouse;
The stockings were hung by the chimney with care,
In hopes that St. Nicholas soon would be there;
The children were nestled all snug in their beds,
While visions of sugar-plums danced in their heads;
And mamma in her 'kerchief, and I in my cap,
Had just settled our brains for a long winter's nap—
When out on the lawn there arose such a clatter,
I sprang from my bed to see what was the matter.
Away to the window I flew like a flash,
Tore open the shutters and threw up the sash.
The moon, on the breast of the new-fallen snow,
Gave a lustre of midday to objects below;
When, what to my wondering eyes should appear,
But a miniature sleigh and eight tiny reindeer,

With a little old driver, so lively and quick,
I knew in a moment it must be St. Nick.
More rapid than eagles his coursers they came,
And he whistled, and shouted, and called them by name:
"Now, *Dasher!* now, *Dancer!* now *Prancer!* and *Vixen!*
On, *Comet!* on, *Cupid!* on *Donner* and *Blitzen!*
To the top of the porch! to the top of the wall!
Now dash away! dash away! dash away all!"
As dry leaves that before the wild hurricane fly,
When they meet with an obstacle, mount to the sky,
So up to the house-top the coursers they flew
With the sleigh full of toys, and St. Nicholas too,
And then, in a twinkling, I heard on the roof
The prancing and pawing of each little hoof—
As I drew in my head, and was turning around,
Down the chimney St. Nicholas came with a bound.
He was dressed all in fur, from his head to his foot,
And his clothes were all tarnished with ashes and soot;
A bundle of toys he had flung on his back,
And he looked like a pedlar just opening his pack.

His eyes—how they twinkled; his dimples, how merry!
His cheeks were like roses, his nose like a cherry!
His droll little mouth was drawn up like a bow,
And the beard of his chin was a white as the snow;
The stump of a pipe he held tight in his teeth,
And the smoke it encircled his head like a wreath;
He had a broad face and a little round belly,
That shook when he laughed, like a bowl full of jelly.
He was chubby and plump, a right jolly old elf,
And I laughed when I saw him, in spite of myself.
A wink of his eye and a twist of his head
Soon gave me to know I had nothing to dread;
He spoke not a word, but went straight to his work,
And filled all the stockings; then turned with a jerk,
And laying his finger aside of his nose,
And giving a nod, up the chimney he rose;
He sprang to his sleigh, to his team gave a whistle,
And away they all flew like the down of a thistle.
But I heard him exclaim, ere he drove out of sight,
"Happy Christmas to all, and to all a good night!"

Christmas Decorations

The oldest Christmas tree ornaments were the edible ones in seventeenth-century German homes. By the nineteenth century, tree decoration with edible and non-edible objects was in full swing. Let little hands make these ornaments and join in the tradition!

GLITTER STARS

*wax paper, glue, glitter
or confetti, scissors, string*

1. Draw stars with glue on a sheet of wax paper and fill in the shapes with a thin layer of glue.
2. Sprinkle glitter or confetti on the glue shapes.
3. Allow to dry; cut out stars.
4. To hang stars, pierce a small hole in the end of one point and loop a piece of string through it.

PAPER CHAIN

scissors, multicolored construction paper, markers, glitter, glue

1. Cut several 5-inch strips of paper. Try cutting zig-zaggy, squiggly, and wavy edges.
2. Decorate with markers or glitter.
3. Glue one strip closed into a ring.
4. Thread another strip into the first ring, then glue shut.
5. Continue connecting rings until the chain is as long as desired. Use as streamers or as tree decoration.

STOCKING ORNAMENT

red construction paper, scissors, tape, hole puncher, yarn, markers, glue, cotton balls

1. Cut same-sized stocking shapes from 2 pieces of paper and tape edges, except the top, together.
2. Punch a hole at the top end and loop yarn through.
3. Write name and decorate with markers.
4. Glue cotton balls around top of stocking.
5. Insert notes, pictures, sticker, or other little surprises into stocking and hang on tree.

Over the River and Through the Woods

O - ver the riv - er and through the woods, To grand-fa-ther's house we
go; _____ The horse knows the way to car - ry the sleigh, Through the
white and drift - ing snow. _____ O - ver the riv - er and
through the woods, Oh how the wind does blow! _____ It stings the toes and
bites the nose as o - ver the ground we go.

Real Me

Susan Cheever

Sarah was my first child and my parents' first granddaughter, two facts that seemed to provoke stuffed animal-buying orgies on the part of otherwise sensible people. My brother Fred and his wife sent her a stuffed brown bear with a white nose and tummy and a manufacturer's name tag that told us his name was "Snuffles." Snuffles joined the piles of plush bears, dogs, cats, frogs, and clowns in her room. Slowly, as Sarah grew and learned to grab, cuddle, and express preferences, she gravitated toward Snuffles. As soon as she could gesture, she let us know that Snuffles needed to be in her crib at night. She began regularly falling asleep with her tiny hands nestling in his soft fur. Like all first mothers, I had read every baby book from Dr. Spock and Penelope Leach to Margaret Mahler, and I knew that the bear was Sarah's transitional object. I was proud of everything Sarah did, and settling on such an appealing transitional object seemed further evidence of her exceptional intelligence.

Of course she didn't call him Snuffles; she was ten months old and innocent of the silly names provided by manufacturers for their products. She didn't even realize he was a bear. She thought he was a cat and she called him Meow, which she shortened to Me. Me the bear became her most beloved thing, the center of her secure world. "Where's my Me?" she would ask, in her sweet little voice. "Where's Me?"

What the baby books forgot to mention was the devastating effect

of too much love. By the time Sarah was two years old, Me was worn and tattered from being caressed, his once gleaming fur had been fondled to a dull, tufted fabric, his eyes were missing and his smile kissed away. After a city-wide hunt, I located another Me— a new Snuffles—and brought him home triumphantly. Sarah was less than pleased. She added the new bear to her menagerie and continued to sleep with the worn-out old one, amending his name to "Real Me" to distinguish him from the imposter.

By the time Sarah turned three, Real Me was a sorry sight. I had changed too. Sarah's love had worn me out and worn me in as it blew my old opinions and preferences to smithereens— to say nothing of my once elegant wardrobe. Coherent outfits became a fond memory as exhaustion drew circles under my eyes and anxiety lined my formerly gleaming skin. As he became more tattered, Real Me seemed to become more necessary— especially after Sarah gave up the bottle which had lulled her to sleep. She couldn't even think about bedtime until Real Me was ensconced on her pillow. When we traveled, Real Me was the first thing I packed. As he crumbled, my anxieties soared. What if he were lost? What if he just came apart at the seams one day after a particularly passionate hug? I was convinced that if that happened Sarah would never sleep again. When I slept I sometimes had nightmares about Real Me. In my dreams he disappeared or disintegrated as I watched helplessly. My psychiatrist asked if I thought my marriage was disintegrating. But if necessity is the mother of invention, mothers are inventors from necessity. One day, shopping in a downtown department store, the escalator took me past the toy department. There, displayed as if he were meant for me to see, was a new Snuffles. I bought him with my heart pounding and had him wrapped in plain brown paper. That night while Sarah slept peacefully, I massacred this new Snuffles with a pair of scissors, reducing him to parts—eyes, nose, ears, and swatches of fur. I crept into Sarah's bedroom and stealthily took Real Me from her pillow. With an ear cocked toward the room where she innocently dreamed, I hastily sewed on one new plush leg.

I didn't sleep at all that night. Had I changed the thing my daughter cared about the most, and ruined it forever? Had I failed to respect her feelings for the one object in the household which belonged to her and her alone? Had I tampered with her sense of security?

Would she notice and be horrified? The next morning I held my breath. Sarah didn't comment. That night at bedtime, I watched terrified as she stroked the new leg in her sleepy ritual. "Mmmm, soft," she said.

After that, every few weeks, I replaced a tiny part of Real Me with a part from the new Snuffles. I have continued to replace parts of Real Me with dozens of parts from new Snuffles I have bought over the years. An eye, a new mouth, a patch of fur, another plush leg—like the human body, Real Me's body has been continually regenerating itself for the last decade. After a few years, Sarah realized what was happening, but by then my replacement rituals had become as much a part of Real Me as the bear himself, and she accepted the fact that Real Me was a patchwork of old and new.

Real Me sits on my computer as I write this, one-eyed and tattered, his tail all but worn off, his neck a shredded patch of fabric. It's been a few years since I have replaced a part. As he is fondled less, he wears better. Sarah is away this weekend, staying with her father (our marriage *was* disintegrating), going to the movies with friends, shopping. These days Real Me sleeps at the end of her bed in a pile of quilts. She doesn't notice him much, and when she leaves she doesn't take him with her. Her security comes from other things now. For her, his usefulness is over. I still keep him, though. I watched him change from the glossy Snuffles—a bear who was as heartless as he was conventional—to the very special, very worn-out Real Me.

For me, Real Me is a testament to the transformative power of the love between mothers and babies. I'll never again be the self-contained girl who thought it might be fun to have a baby. I'll never be able to leave home so blithely; I never walk out the door without feeling a piece of my heart has been left behind. My daughter's birth and the strain of raising her has irreparably damaged the young body which once brought me so much pleasure. Looking back, however, I would say that I didn't know what pleasure was then. Real Me and I are a pair. A child's love wore him out, a child's love repaired and mended him, a child's love made him old and interesting and precious. Come to think of it, that's just what happened to me.

❋

Ellen H. Clapsadle

Paper Dolls

It is not uncommon for young children to ask constantly for more of this or more of that. Now you can give them as many dolls as you can fold and cut out. Try cutting gingerbread men or teddy bear chains as well.

a long sheet of paper, pencil,
scissors, crayons, extra paper, glue

1. Fold the paper lengthwise in fourths or eighths.
2. Draw the outline of a doll on the top fold. Extend the hands to both edges of the paper so the dolls will "hold hands" and remain connected.
3. Cut along the outline and unfold the paper to reveal a chain of paper dolls.
4. Draw different faces, hair, clothing, and accessories with crayons.
5. Cut out different shapes for hats and shoes to glue on.

When I Grow Up
William Wise

When I grow up,
I think I'll be
A detective
With a skeleton key.

I could be a soldier
And a sailor too;
I'd like to be a keeper
At the public zoo.

I'll own a trumpet
And I'll play a tune;
I'll keep a space ship
To explore the moon.

I'll be a cowboy
And live in the saddle;
I'll be a guide
With a canoe and a paddle.

I'd like to be the driver
On a diesel train;
And it must be fun
To run a building crane.

I'll live in a lighthouse
And guard the shore;
And I know I'll want to be
A dozen things more.

For the more a boy lives
The more a boy learns—
I think I'll be all of them
By taking turns.

Peter Pan

J. M. Barrie

All children, except one, grow up. They soon know that they will grow up, and the way Wendy knew was this. One day when she was two years old she was playing in a garden, and she plucked another flower and ran with it to her mother. I suppose she must have looked rather delightful, for Mrs. Darling put her hand to her heart and cried, 'Oh, why can't you remain like this for ever!' This was all that passed between them on the subject, but henceforth Wendy knew that she must grow up. You always know after you are two. Two is the beginning of the end. . . .

Wendy came first, then John, then Michael.

For a week or two after Wendy came it was doubtful whether they would be able to keep her, as she was another mouth to feed. . . .

There was the same excitement over John, and Michael had even a narrower squeak; but both were kept, and soon you might have seen the three of them going in a row to Miss Fulsom's Kindergarten school, accompanied by their nurse.

Mrs. Darling loved to have everything just so, and Mr. Darling had a passion for being exactly like his neighbours; so, of course, they had a nurse. As they were poor, owing to the amount of milk the children drank, this nurse was a prim Newfoundland dog,

called Nana who had belonged to no one in particular until the Darlings engaged her. She had always thought children important, however, and the Darlings had become acquainted with her in Kensington Gardens, where she spent most of her spare time peeping into perambulators, and was much hated by careless nursemaids, whom she followed to their homes and complained of to their mistresses. She proved to be quite a treasure of a nurse. How thorough she was at bathtime; and up at any moment of the night if one of charges made the slightest cry. Of course, her kennel was in the nursery. She had a genius for knowing when a cough is a thing to have no patience with and when it needs stocking around your throat. She believed to her last day in old-fashioned remedies like rhubarb leaf, and made sounds of contempt over all this new-fangled talk about germs, and so on. It was a lesson

in propriety to see her escorting the children to school, walking sedately by their side when they were well behaved, and butting them back into line if they strayed. On John's soccer days she never once forgot his sweater, and she usually carried an umbrella in her mouth in case of rain. There is a room in the basement of Miss Fulsom's school where the nurses wait. They sat on forms, while Nana lay on the floor, but that was the only difference. They affected to ignore her as of an inferior social status to themselves, and she despised their light talk. She resented visits to the nursery from Mrs. Darling's friends, but if they did come she first whipped off Michael's pinafore and put him into the one with blue braiding, and smoothed out Wendy and made a dash at John's hair.

Mrs. Darling first heard of Peter when she was tidying up her children's minds. It is the nightly custom of every good mother after her children are asleep to rummage in their minds and put things straight for next morning, repacking into their proper places the many articles that have wandered during the day. If you could keep awake (but of course you can't) you would see your own mother doing this, and you would find it very interesting to watch her. It is quite like tidying up drawers. You would see her on her knees, I expect, lingering humorously over some of your contents, wondering where on earth you had picked this thing up, making discoveries sweet and not so sweet, pressing this to her cheek as if it were as nice as a kitten, and hurriedly stowing that out of sight. When you wake in the morning, the naughtiness and evil passions with which you went to bed have been folded up small and placed at the bottom of your mind; and on the top, beautifully aired, are spread out your prettier thoughts, ready for you to put on.

Occasionally in her travels through her children's minds Mrs. Darling found things she could not understand, and of these quite the most perplexing was the word Peter. She knew of no Peter, and yet he was here and there in John and Michael's minds, while Wendy's began to be scrawled all over with him. The name stood out in bolder letters than any of the other words, and as Mrs. Darling gazed she felt that it had an oddly cocky appearance.

"Yes, he is rather cocky," Wendy admitted with regret. Her mother had been questioning her.

"But who is he, my pet?"

"He is Peter Pan, you know, mother."

❀

I kiss you and kiss you,
With arms round my own,
Ah, how shall I miss you,
When, dear, you have grown.

—William Butler Yeats

Ten Blocks

Terry Strother

I love traveling with my daughter. At neighborhood playgrounds she watches, watches. She will carefully climb up the ladder of the slide and climb back down again, cautious, slow. Who, then, is this daredevil who, when traveling, practically runs up mountains? Who delights in clambering over slippery riverbed rocks, finding and losing and finding her balance? I marveled once at the image of her tiny body astride the bare back of a Belgian workhorse. When I went to mount behind her, she firmly declined, then added gently, "Don't worry, Mama." But the distance we travel most together is the ten city blocks between our home and Emma's pre-school. In this well-traveled place, my daughter is my teacher.

It's a school morning, grey and drizzly, and we have all overslept. Nevertheless, I'm trying to keep things moving along. Perhaps I'll still be able to get my daughter to school in time for "circle time," her favorite part of the day.

Emma is newly four. Developmentally speaking, four equals oppositional. That's how she figures out that she's not her parents but a separate, unique individual. That's her job. My job, as I see it at the moment, is to accomplish certain tasks of living in spite of this.

I go to brush Emma's hair as she's eating breakfast. She jumps up and runs out of the room as I call after her disappearing form: "Please do *not* run away." The door slams. I don't have time for this. I'm pissed. I find her on my bed, snatch her up, and carry her the length of the apartment back to

the breakfast table where her small but clear voice says: "Don't set me down with a bump."

It registers. She's afraid of my anger—which immediately softens. We negotiate the brushing of the hair. She is a force to be reckoned with. Frustration moves in—why does everything have to be negotiated? Just once can't we just get something done efficiently? She's a kid; it shouldn't be this complicated. Besides, she's the one who'll be disappointed to miss circle time. In the end she's distracted and not eating breakfast. When I remind her we need to hurry a bit she says: "Can we have one more slow day before we go back to fast days?"

My heart breaks. This is what the resistance is about—not what happens, but how it happens. Slowly, without agendas. It's understandable considering this is only her second day back at school after a bout of pneumonia. The transition is too abrupt. I realize how unavailable I have been, my thoughts preoccupied with concern over Emma's physical health.

"We can have as many slow days as you want . . ."

"I want five." She holds up fingers.

". . . but the slower you go the more important it is to be mindful and direct when something needs to get done."

"But my mind is jumping around like a monkey—it's here now. Oh, now it's here . . ." She points to different parts of her head.

"When your mind jumps away, you can bring it back by saying—where am I?"

She is surprised. "At the table."

"What am I doing?"

"Eating breakfast."

"How do I do it?" (puzzled look)

She looks puzzled. "Pick up the spoon."

Laughter. Takes a bite.

It becomes a game and we make it through breakfast this way—where am I? what am I doing? how do I do it? Meanwhile, it's now pouring rain outside. I'm thinking I can make up some time by getting a cab to school this morning instead of walking. Obviously I'm desperate. Emma soon makes it clear she doesn't want to take a cab. Quick, choose, is this a battle worth fighting? Naw, I really don't want to either. It's not so bad out, really, just very wet.

Out on the sidewalk I find that I can't hold an umbrella and push a stroller at the same time. I think of insisting that Emma sit in the stroller and that we "run between the raindrops" to school but something stops me. I turn and look back. Emma is smiling as she walks: big confident strides, umbrella cocked back, rain boots squishing.

Then I realize what she's doing: where am I?—on the sidewalk; what am I doing?—walking in the rain; how do I do it?—put one foot in front of the other. Or some version of that.

At any rate she is fully in the moment, in her environment, and thoroughly enjoying it.

The sensation of the umbrella bumping against a railing brings delighted laughter. Each puddle is a pond, or a rushing stream, depending on its nature. She's absorbed in the details. We find a "pirate key" in the mud at the base of an old gnarled tree and, up the street, a tiny sign precariously perched on the edge of a gutter that says "squirrel." Obviously a clue. We need only find squirrel island on a map to know where to look for the pirate's treasure. A sanitation truck rumbles by. I join Emma in waving to the driver who, impishly, smiles back as he flips us the finger.

Ah, New York. Emma, of course, has no idea the meaning of this particular gesture. She's moved on and is now making "a present" out of things she has found: a few buds freed by last night's storm, bits of colorful plastic, and a bottle cap, together with a mound of mud.

~

The care she's taking with her arrangement suddenly reminds me of a similar activity in Bali. The Balinese make little offerings that they place outside of their homes and at cross-

roads two times during the day to appease the evil spirits. These offerings are tiny banana leaf constructions filled with flowers, fruit, rice, and incense. Each one is a miracle of color and placement. As the hours go by, the offerings are squashed by feet and motorcycles, poked at by dogs and chickens, hopefully satiating the evil spirits. While traveling there, I remember loving the idea that, at least once a day, you devote your energy to making something beautiful, making something calm and spellbinding enough to quell the stirrings of the most unsettled spirits. This way even if bad things do happen, you are secure in knowing that you have done your best to calm the storm. As if aware of my thoughts, Emma looks up from her creation: "When people die they become the moons over different countries, but their spirits stay here and they like to see pretty things."

The stroller's too bulky to fold up and carry, so by the time we reach school a sizable puddle has formed in the seat and I'm drenched. Emma's wet in front from the sling-back approach to carrying her umbrella. But for the last three or four blocks she's been singing . . .

Drip drip drop
little April showers
what can compare with your
    beautiful sound
beautiful sound
beautiful sound?

We missed circle time. But, of course, we almost missed a lot more. The teacher greets us and says, "She looks really good today, really healthy."

She is. She is.

❊

CLASSIC COOKIES

Here are recipes for three all-time favorite cookies. Let little hands help with the mixing and spooning. Keep the cookie jar filled with any one of this trio and you will be sure to keep smiles on little faces.

CHOCOLATE CHIP COOKIES

$2^1/4$ cups all-purpose flour
1 teaspoon baking soda
$1/4$ teaspoon salt
$3/4$ cup brown sugar
$3/4$ cup white sugar
$1^1/4$ cups ($2^1/2$ sticks) unsalted butter, softened
1 cup chopped walnuts (optional)
2 cups (12 ounces) semi-sweet chocolate chips
2 eggs, slightly beaten (use 3 eggs for crispier cookies)
1 teaspoon vanilla extract

1. Preheat oven to 375°F.
2. Combine flour, baking soda, salt, and sugars and mix well.
3. Using your fingers, mix in the butter until mixture is crumbly. Add nuts and chips.
4. Beat eggs and vanilla together, then add to the cookie mixture and blend.
5. Using a tablespoon, drop small mounds (you should be able to fit 16 cookies on a sheet at a time) onto an ungreased cookie sheet.
6. Bake for 10–12 minutes or until brown. Remove from hot sheet immediately.
   Makes about 4 dozen small cookies

OATMEAL RAISIN COOKIES

2 sticks (1 cup) butter, softened
1 cup packed brown sugar
$1/2$ cup sugar
2 eggs

1 teaspoon vanilla extract
1 1/2 cups all-purpose flour
1 teaspoon baking soda
1 teaspoon ground cinnamon
1/2 teaspoon salt (optional)
3 cups quick-cooking rolled oats
1 cup raisins

1. Preheat oven to 350°F.
2. Grease a cookie sheet or lay a sheet of parchment paper on it.
3. In a large bowl, cream together butter and sugars until light.
4. Add eggs and vanilla. Beat well.
5. In a separate bowl, combine flour, baking soda, cinnamon, and salt and gradually add to the butter mixture. Mix well.
6. Fold in oats and raisins. Mix well.
7. Drop mixture onto cookie sheet, one tablespoon at a time, around 2 inches apart. Bake 10–12 minutes until lightly browned.
8. Transfer cookies to wire racks and let cool.

Makes about 4 dozen cookies

PEANUT BUTTER COOKIES

1/2 cup honey
1/2 cup crunchy peanut butter
1/2 stick of butter, softened
1 egg
1 cup all-purpose white flour
1/4 teaspoon baking powder
pinch of salt

1. Preheat oven to 375°F.
2. Grease a cookie sheet or lay a sheet of parchment paper on it.
3. Put honey, peanut butter, butter, and egg in mixing bowl and beat with an electric mixer for 2 minutes (or just beat well by hand).
4. In a separate bowl, combine flour, baking powder, and salt and gradually add to the peanut butter mixture. Mix well.
5. Drop mixture onto cookie sheet one teaspoon at a time, around 2 inches apart. Bake 12–15 minutes until lightly browned.
6. Transfer cookies to wire racks and let cool.

Makes about 2 dozen cookies

Little Boy Blue, come,
blow your horn!

The sheep's in the meadow,
the cow's in the corn.

Where's the little boy that
looks after the sheep?

Boy Blue

Under the
haystack,
fast asleep!

Sleeping Beauty

Once upon a time there were a King and Queen whose castle sat atop a magic mountain, where all the fairies of the land were said to live in hidden caves.

One day, the Queen gave birth to her first child, a daughter, and named her Bella, which means "beautiful." The King wished to have his baby daughter blessed by each of the ten fairies that lived on the mountain, and sent a messenger boy to invite them all to a celebration in honor of Bella's birth.

Though he searched beneath each rock and climbed up every tree, the messenger boy could find only nine of the fairies, and hence returned to the castle in fear he would be punished. So afraid the King would be angry with him, the boy decided not to tell anyone he had failed at his task.

The day of the celebration arrived, and the King and Queen were overjoyed so much so that they did not even notice one fairy was missing. Beaming with pride, they presented their daughter, swathed in the finest silk and lace, to their guests. One by one, each fairy stepped forward and blessed Bella with a gift.

The first fairy blessed her with eternal beauty. The second fairy blessed her with great intelligence. The third fairy blessed her with a wonderful sense of humor. The fourth fairy blessed her with perfect health. The fifth fairy blessed her with genuine compassion. The sixth fairy blessed her with an adventurous spirit. The seventh fairy blessed her with creativity. The eighth fairy blessed her with unconditional kindness.

Just as the ninth fairy stepped forward to bestow her blessing, a loud commotion was heard from the back of the hall. Suddenly, a very old fairy pushed her way through the crowd till she stood right in front of the King and Queen.

"How dare you not invite me to bless your firstborn child?! You disgust me!" she spat at the royal couple.

"But of course you were invited," said the shocked King, "I sent my messenger boy to personally ask all the fairies to join our celebration!" Then the King turned to his courtiers and demanded, "Bring me the messenger! I wish to speak with him immediately!" But strangely enough, the young boy appeared to absent from the festivities. . . .

"Lies!" accused the fairy, "you're full of lies! Well, I shall make you pay for your insult by giving your daughter a very *special* blessing." With that, the old fairy placed her hand on the Princess's forehead and uttered, "I, the fairy of mortality, decree that this child will prick her finger on a spindle in her sixteenth year and fall dead in an instant, along with any living thing inside these castle walls." The Queen let out an anguished sob.

"Maybe," snapped the old fairy as she left the room, "you'll think better next time before you show me such discourtesy!"

Just then, the ninth fairy stepped forward and offered sympathetically, "My dear King and Queen, I cannot undue this terrible curse, but I can temper it." The fairy placed a hand on baby Bella's head and continued, "Do not let this child, nor any other living soul, die by the prick of a spindle, but fall fast asleep for a hundred years, instead."

The King thanked the fairy for her kindness, and further decreed that all the sewing spindles in his kingdom be taken away and burned to ashes.

Years passed, and Princess Bella grew to be a gentle, kind, intelligent, and beautiful young woman. On her sixteenth birthday, her parents threw her an extravagant party and invited all the people in the land to join them in their celebration. That night, the princess danced her heart out with almost every young man in the kingdom. As the last song of the night was announced, a dashing prince tapped Bella lightly on the shoulder. "Your Highness," he asked politely, "may I have this dance."

As Bella whirled around to answer, she was stunned by the

sight of the young prince standing before her. He had, quite simply, the most lovely eyes she had ever seen.

"Why, I would be honored," she replied with a curtsy.

As the couple waltzed, the dance floor slowly cleared, the other guests unable to do anything but stop and stare. You see, the Prince and Princess moved so beautifully together, it was as if they were one person, swaying and twirling through the room. As the evening came to an end, the Prince bid Bella good night, and asked if he might call on her again. She consented readily, and watched as he rode down the steep mountain slope out of sight.

That night, as the Princess prepared for bed, her mother came in to brush her hair.

"Oh mother," whispered Bella, "something wonderful has happened to me tonight."

"And what might that be?" asked her mother with a knowing smile, for she had seen the way her daughter danced with the handsome Prince.

"I fell in love!" swooned Bella.

The next morning, the Prince's father, the king of a nearby town, called and invited the Princess's parents to visit his castle. He wished to discuss the possibility of a marriage between their children. Bella was dazed with joy and urged her father to make a good impression and not be too stern with the Prince

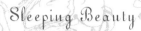

Sleeping Beauty

or his family. As she waved good-bye to the King and Queen, Bella felt warm, wet, tears stream down her cheeks. These were the happiest of tears, and she called out to her parents that she loved them both and wished them a safe trip.

Alone, with neither the King nor Queen to watch over her, the curious Bella decided to explore a tower in the castle that had always been declared "off limits" to her. As she climbed the narrow staircase leading to the tower's uppermost room, the Princess heard a soft clicking that grew louder as she approached the top step. Cautiously, she opened a heavy wooden door and discovered an old woman sitting at a spindle, quietly sewing some linens. As Bella approached her, the old lady looked up and smiled. "Would you like to try my spindle?" she asked kindly.

Bella quickly agreed and walked toward the spindle. But as she sat down, her pinkie finger grazed the spindle's needle and she felt a tiny prick. Immediately, the Princess's eyelids drooped and she fell slowly off the stool, landing softly on the floor. The sleeping spell spread quickly throughout the castle, and every scullery maid, cook, courtier, knight, dog, cat, and goldfish fell fast asleep where they stood (or swam!). The old fairy's curse had finally come true, and the beautiful Princess, along with her royal staff, were to lay sleeping for a hundred years.

The King and Queen wept bitterly when they learned of their

daughter's fate. They decided to leave the castle just as it was, frozen in time, so that when the Princess awoke she would feel at home.

As the years passed, time went forward, except in Bella's castle. The King and Queen, who had moved away to another land, died peacefully in their old age. A new city was built around the magical mountain. No one ever dared enter the ancient castle, in fear they too would fall under the fairy's spell. But a legend was born that the most beautiful princess in the world lay fast asleep in one of the stone towers, and that the fairies looked in on her every evening.

One day, a handsome young Prince rode into town. He had heard the tale of the sleeping Princess who lay in the castle and had come to see her with his own eyes. A local caretaker who lived in a small cottage at the base of the mountain warned the Prince of the curse that would befall any man who stepped foot inside the castle walls. But the Prince would not be deterred from finding the Princess that legend told was the most beautiful and kindest who ever lived.

The Prince reached the mountaintop late in the night, and strode boldly across the drawbridge. Just as he entered the castle, a cuckoo clock chirped loudly signaling the stroke of midnight. At that moment the curse was lifted, for exactly one

century had gone by since the Princess pricked her finger on the spindle. The Prince climbed the staircase to the tower and found Princess Bella still asleep. He knelt over her, gently lifted her head, and kissed her tenderly on the lips. "Wake up my sleeping beauty, wake up," he whispered.

The Princess's eyes fluttered open and she saw above her the face of a man who looked just like the Prince she had fallen in love with a hundred years before. You see, this was the great great great grandson of the Prince who had stolen Bella's heart on her sixteenth birthday.

Bella yawned and smiled at the young Prince. "I must have fallen asleep while I was sewing. Did your father accept my dowry? Am I to be your bride?"

"Oh I hope so," replied the love-struck Prince. "But I am not the man you think I am." And he told the Princess of how long she had slept and how the world had both changed and stayed the same while she'd been slumbering.

The Princess was confused at first, and quite heartbroken to hear of her parents' death. But in time, she became happy again, as she once had been. She fell deeply in love with the Prince who had woken her, just as she had with his great great great grand-father. Before long, the Prince and Princess married and lived happily ever after in their castle on the magic mountain. ❀

Hush, Little Baby

Hush lit-tle ba-by, don't say a word,

Pa-pa's gon-na buy you a mock-ing bird. And

if that mock-ing bird won't sing,

Pa-pa's gon-na buy you a dia-mond ring. __

2. If that mockingbird don't sing,
Papa's gonna buy you a diamond ring.

3. If that diamond ring turns to brass,
Papa's gonna buy you a looking glass.

4. If that looking glass gets broke,
Papa's gonna buy you a billy goat.

5. If that billy goat don't pull,
Papa's gonna buy you a cart and bull.

6. If that cart and bull turn over,
Papa's gonna buy you a dog named Rover.

7. If that dog named Rover don't bark,
Papa's gonna buy you a horse and cart.

8. If that horse and cart fall down,
You'll still be the sweetest little baby in town.

Vespers
A. A. Milne

Little Boy kneels at the foot of the bed,
Droops on the little hands little gold head.
Hush! Hush! Whisper who dares!
Christopher Robin is saying his prayers.

God bless Mummy. I know that's right.
Wasn't it fun in the bath tonight?
The cold's so cold, and the hot's so hot.
Oh! *God bless Daddy*—I quite forgot.

If I open my fingers a little bit more,
I can see Nanny's dressing-gown on the door.
It's a beautiful blue, but it hasn't a hood.
Oh! *God bless Nanny and make her good.*

Mine has a hood, and I lie in bed,
And pull the hood right over my head,
And I shut my eyes, and I curl up small,
And nobody knows that I'm there at all.

Oh! *Thank you, God, for a lovely day.*
And what was the other I had to say?
I said "Bless Daddy," so what can it be?
Oh! *Now I remember. God bless Me.*

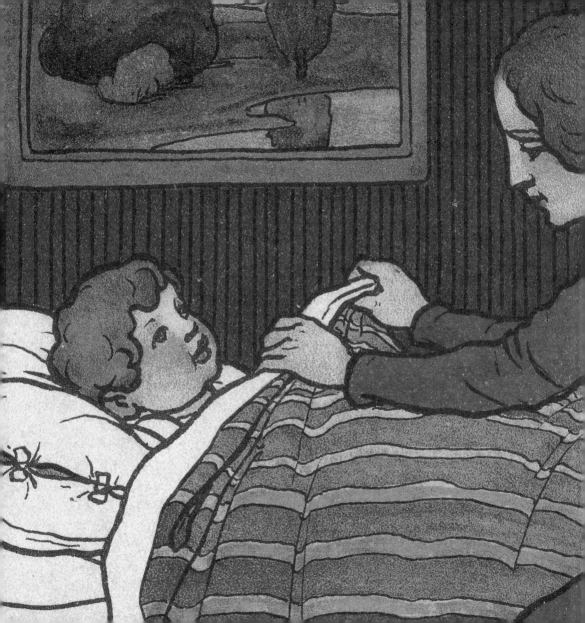

Acknowledgments

"Life Doesn't Frighten Me" from *And Still I Rise* by Maya Angelou. Copyright © 1978 by Maya Angelou. Reprinted by permission of Random House, Inc. and Virago Press UK.

"Real Me" copyright © Susan Cheever. Reprinted by permission of the author.

"maggie and milly and molly and may" copyright © 1956, 1984, 1991 by the Trustees for the E. E. Cummings Trust, from *Complete Poems: 1904–1962* by E. E. Cummings, edited by George J. Firmage. Reprinted by permission of Liveright Publishing Corporation.

"The Old Man Who Said 'Why?'" from *Fairy Tales* by E. E. Cummings. Copyright © 1965, 1993 by the Trustees for the E. E. Cummings Trust. Reprinted by permission of Liveright Publishing Corporation.

"A Dangerous Thing to Hope For" copyright © 1997 by Gail Grenier. Reprinted by permission of the author.

"Baby Feet" from *The Collected Verse of Edgar A. Guest*. Copyright © 1934. Reprinted by permission of Contemporary Books.

"Mortal Terrors and Motherhood" copyright © Amy Herrick. Reprinted by permission of the author.

"IF" by Rudyard Kipling. Reprinted by permission of A. P. Watt Limited on behalf of The National Trust for Places of Historic Interest or Natural Beauty.

"Operating Instructions" by Anne Lamott. Copyright © 1994 by Anne Lamott. Reprinted by permission of Pantheon Books, a division of Random House, Inc.

"Vespers" by A. A. Milne, from *When We Were Very Young* by A. A. Milne, illustrations by E. H. Shepard, copyright 1924 by E. P. Dutton, renewed 1952 by A. A. Milne. Used by permission of Dutton Children's Books, a division of Penguin Putnam Inc. Permission for the British Commonwealth: From *When We Were Very Young* by A. A. Milne. Copyright under the Berne Convention. Published by Methuen, an imprint of Egmont Children's Books Limited, London.
"Adventures of Isabel" by Ogden Nash. Copyright © 1936 by Ogden Nash. By permission of Little, Brown and Company, Inc. and André Deutsch.

"Sick" from *Where the Sidewalk Ends* by Shel Silverstein. Copyright © 1974 by Evil Eye Music, Inc. Reprinted with permission of HarperCollins Publishing, Inc., and by permission of Edite Kroll Literary Agency.

"Ten Blocks" by Terry Strother. Copyright © Terry Strother. From *Traveler's Tales: A Mother's World*, Bond & Michael, eds. Travelers Tales, Inc., San Francisco, 1998. Reprinted by permission of the author.

Charlotte's Web © 1952 by E. B. White. Renewed 1980 by E. B. White. Reprinted by permission of HarperCollins Publishers.

"When I Grow Up" from *Jonathan Blake* by William Wise. Copyright © 1956, 1984 by William Wise. Reprinted by permission of Curtis Brown Ltd., New York.

"I kiss you, I kiss you…" from "A Cradle Song" by W. B. Yeats. Reprinted with the permission of Scribner, a Division of Simon & Schuster. From *The Poems of W. B. Yeats: A New Edition*, edited by Richard J. Finneran. Copyright © 1983 by Anne Yeats.

ILLUSTRATION CREDITS:

Cover and back, pg. 1, 2, 3: Hilda Austin; pg. 6: George T. Tobis; pg. 10: Nina K. Brisley; pg. 17: Annie Benson Muller; pg. 24: Pauli Ebner; pg. 27, 187: R. Caldecott; pg. 40: Magnus Greiner; pg. 42–43, 190–191, 228-229, 270, 271, 314–315: Ida Waugh; pg. 55, 194, 195: R. H. Porteous; pg. 84–85: F. Bisel Peat; pg. 88, 212, 213: Eul Alie; pg. 91: E. C. Pauli and Roberts; pg. 98: M. E. Edwards; pg. 119: E. Dorothy Rees; pg. 120: Anita Purkurst; pg. 124–125: M.E.P.; pg. 127, 319: Ruth Cobb; pg. 128: Maxfield Parrish; pg. 145: Frances Brundage; pg. 147: C. M. Burd; pg. 154: Louise C. Rumoty; pg. 159: Blanche Fischer Wright; pg. 162–163: E. Faimiloe; pg. 174: Gordon Robinson; pg. 177: Mary Anderson; pg. 207: Florence Harrison; pg. 210: R. J. Lunt Roberts; pg. 232: E. Ridgway; pg. 243: Maginal Wright Barney; pg. 301: Torre Bevasio; pg. 306: Agnes Richardson; pg. 311: H.Q.C. Marsh; pg. 313: Ellen H. Clapsaddle; pg. 327: Jessie Willcox Smith; pg. 330: G. G. Weidergeim; pg. 347: A. Aein.